Interpreting the Bible Today

R.E.O. White

S 191

Pickering & Inglis Ltd.
LONDON · GLASGOW

Copyright © R.E.O. White 1982

ISBN 0 7208 0500 7
Cat. No. 01/0912

First printing 1982

Contents

1

The Need for Guidelines

'But that is only your interpretation. I understand the Bible differently.'

How many promising Christian conversations have been brought to an abrupt end by that retort. All serious discussion, all responsible appeal to scripture for illumination or authority, and all hope of Christian agreement, are rendered futile when every man's interpretation is held to be as valid as every other man's. The Bible is then not worth quoting.

Three hundred and fifty modern versions in English alone have helped to create this impasse. They cannot all be correct; so many attempts suggest that no one can get the translation right, and where scholars manifestly disagree anyone is entitled to try his hand. The resulting confusion is, to all who love the word of God, little short of disastrous.

'The Bible,' said Chillingworth in the seventeenth century, 'and the Bible only, is the religion of Protestants.' In our time, while scripture holds an increasingly honoured place in the Roman and Orthodox churches, among Protestant sects its authority has greatly declined, largely because of disagreement over what the Bible means, and the widespread claim to 'the right of private interpretation'. Such a situation cries aloud for safeguards, guidelines, in the right and reverent use of scripture.

But cannot Christian people, with the Bible in their hands, be left to read it for themselves, without officious mentors telling them how to understand it? In the end, yes. Each reader must bear his own responsibility for what he makes of God's word, and for how he responds to it. He can delegate to no one else, whether priest, pastor, scholar, or friend, the duty of discovering what God is saying to his own soul. But that is no reason why he should not seek to become informed and competent in his handling of so powerful, and so dangerous, a book as the Christian Bible.

For not all who value the Bible are wise or consistent in their use of it. Most of us are highly *selective* in what we choose to count important, without thinking too much about the reasons for our preference. How many could say, at once, why they obey literally, at the Lord's Supper, the command 'Do this in remembrance of me' (1 Cor. 11:24), and ignore 'You also ought to wash one another's feet' (John 13:14), spoken across the same table?

Or, why we quote so earnestly, 'Remember the sabbath day, to keep it holy', and keep the first day, not the sabbath? Why, seeking a scriptural pattern of worship, do some of us turn only to the priesthood of the Old Testament, and others only to the troubled church at Corinth? Why do we faithfully end our services with the Benediction, but rarely begin them, as Paul suggests, by greeting one another with a holy kiss (1 Cor. 16:20)? And why do so many remember with scrupulous care what Paul apparently wrote about women keeping silent in the church, and have not noticed either the promise of the Spirit of prophecy to 'daughters and handmaidens' (Acts 2:17,18), or the praying and prophesying by women in public which Paul elsewhere refers to (1 Cor. 11:5)?

The Bible contains innumerable commands and exhortations which modern Christians choose to ignore, from those concerning 'unclean meats', animal sacrifices, tithing and circumcision to those prohibiting 'religious' dress, 'religious' titles, the taking of oaths, the confusion of male and female clothing, and many more. We are all inconsistent in this way, in our 'loyalty to scripture' casually and almost unconsciously deciding what is still binding upon the Christian conscience, while criticising sharply any whose choice of what to obey differs from our own.

News out of modern China underlines the danger of *private* interpretation — the warning that 'no prophecy of scripture is a matter of one's own interpretation' (2 Pet. 1:20). Describing the effects of years of public disfavour upon the Chinese church, Bishop Ting has said that in going underground the Chinese Christians have fostered small house-groups in place of the banned public services. The tenacity, courage, and faith in the future thus demonstrated are beyond praise. But — so it appears — a price has been paid. Cut off from 'the commerce of Christian thought' in the wider church, from the fruits of agelong study of the scriptures, and from the sifting process of discussion, such groups have seized upon particular and partial truths, ideas, stories, duties, and exaggerated their significance beyond all due proportion, neglecting other truths and duties in consequence.

Details are not given, but house-groups in the western churches, with nothing like the justification which harassed Chinese Christians could plead, have had similar experience. Individual Christians, too, sometimes become unbalanced and obsessed with their own private interpretation of some passage which has struck their fancy, to the great hindrance of their spiritual growth and usefulness.

It is easy to caricature earnest souls meeting for 'Bible study' who merely pool their 'feelings' about a passage, share each other's ignorance as to what it originally meant, and take a vote on 'what it really means today'. Equally earnest expository preachers sometimes disappoint their hearers because they do not draw from some well-known passage the interpretation and application made familiar by a revered preacher of the past. Quite often it is because the speaker has 'done his homework' and knows that neither its language, its background or its purpose justify that use of the passage.

Two examples will suffice. Many evangelical sermons have been preached upon Jeremiah's visit to the potter's house, sermons which have eloquently described the gentle skill of the divine fingers to reshape a spoiled life to usefulness and beauty. In truth, Jeremiah was insisting on God's right to change his purpose, when people resist his hand, and to 'shape evil' against those he had purposed to love. The passage is one of terrible warning, not of gracious promise (Jer. 18:1–11).

Many urgent appeals have been made to sinners to let Christ into their lives and not keep him standing on the threshold, with help from Holman Hunt's picture of the Light of the World beside a door without an outside latch. This is the traditional homiletic use of the text, 'Behold, I stand at the door and knock; if any one hears my voice and opens the door, I will come in to him and eat with him, and he with me' (Rev. 3:20). But this ignores the plain meaning of the passage, that Christ stands 'rapping' (Greek) at the door of the Laodicean church, demanding to be admitted by the few faithful within.

Jesus himself warns against thus 'making void the word of God through your tradition which you hand on' (Mark 7:13); by thus reading it always with the mental assumptions and footnotes which we inherit from honoured teachers of the past but which nevertheless can hide from us the true meaning of scripture. Of course, the firm guidelines for Bible study which any teacher offers can likewise be no more than his own prejudices and misleading theories, unless they arise from the nature of revelation and the process by which the Bible came to us.

The *superstitious* use of scripture arises mainly from exaggerated reverence for biblical words in themselves. Texts have been used as charms, both worn on the person and in the Christian home. They are quoted sometimes in evangelism and in preaching with a naive confidence that the actual words of the Authorised King James Version have some inherent spiritual power — almost as a form of incantation or spell. Occasionally, this attitude to scripture's actual words, written or spoken, is found among those who would at once cry 'superstition and magic!' against any similar idea of effective spiritual power operating through the Christian sacraments. A similar semi-superstitious regard for the very fabric of the Bible frowns upon the making of marginal notes and the underlining of favourite texts.

Such superstition is more silly than serious: it becomes dangerous with the habit of bringing together words and phrases from widely separated passages and recombining them into new statements without reference to their original setting and meaning, and then claiming that any new combination of 'inspired words' will likewise be 'inspired'. It sounds too stupid to be credible, yet it is done. Some phrases which Isaiah addresses explicitly to the king of Babylon, as 'a man' who made the earth tremble (Isa. 14:4,16), and similar expressions used by Ezekiel of the prince of Tyre (28:2,12) have long been combined with other phrases from Genesis and still others from

Revelation to construct a whole 'pre-history' of Satan, which owes far more to apocryphal books which the church rejected, to the poet Milton, and to misplaced ingenuity than it does to the Bible. Yet many Christians accept it as 'God's word'.

The same method is followed in bringing together scattered prophecies assumed still to await fulfilment, and endlessly re-arranging them to construct programmes of future events which God — we are told — 'must' bring to pass according to 'his word'. The only effect of this attitude towards the words of scripture is to alienate earnest minds from any attempt to understand the Bible.

Equally mischievous is the light-hearted *misapplication* of scripture, to the confusion of the Christian conscience. Paul's exhortation to Christians to 'come out from among' the sensual, drunken, quarrelsome and ungodly in desperately sinful Corinth so that their own Christian discipline shall be safe and their witness clear, has been quoted time and again to urge Christians to leave their present churches to join some schismatic group which thinks itself more faithful to God's word! A Christian leader urged to have care for the spiritual welfare of his own children, often neglected as he pursued his wide ministry, replied, 'I am certain they will grow up right; I believe Christ is able to keep what I have committed unto him' — a misquotation, misapplication, and indefensible irresponsibility all in one, yet 'Bible-based'.

How very often the petition of Jesus, that the disciples may be one as he and the Father are one, has been used to suggest that he was praying for the World Council of Churches, equating the unity within the Trinity with the business efficiency of a world-wide ecclesiastical corporation! In a small booklet on the Spirit and Pentecostalism, it was possible to count eighteen clear instances where the scripture verses cited to support the argument were not merely debatable but wholly irrelevant, the alleged meaning being nowhere in sight.

A Scottish deacon, coming upon the requirement that a deacon should be 'the husband of one wife' immediately resigned, and demanded the resignation of two others who also were single. The four anchors which the sailors cast from the stern of Paul's sinking ship were *not* the Bible, the church, the sacraments and the gospel, which Christians should not throw overboard, in any case.

The temptation to misapply scripture is certainly not new. Saint Cyprian, sixteen centuries ago, castigated 'smooth tongued advocates of vice' who cited Elijah and the chariots of Israel to justify attendance at pagan chariot-competitions; David's dancing before the Ark to justify their own enjoyment of the theatre's lewd spectacles; Paul's allusions to the athletic games to justify their own participation — ignoring, as Cyprian says, the fact that the scriptures themselves forbid such practices.

But then, serious theologians have found support for the doctrine of the Trinity in an idiomatic Hebrew plural verb. They have argued a 'Christian' doctrine of sin from a Jewish psalm, and claimed to find in a passage which deliberately opposes human sacrifice — God's preventing Abraham's offering of Isaac — a prophecy of God's providing a human sacrifice in Jesus. The revered Principal of a famous Bible College, not liking the outcome of the meticulous examination of certain scripture verses, wrote 'I am sure you could get another meaning out of that passage if you tried.' Even the deliberate misuse of scripture is not confined to untutored Christians.

A few far-reaching *distortions* of scripture should be mentioned. An influential evangelical author re-writes the story of the cleansing of the Temple by Jesus, to show there was no whip, no anger or flailing or fear — all that was invented by scholars! Jesus simply picked up a few stray straws and stood silent:

people felt a superstitious awe within the Temple, remembering the old prophets; that mood communicated itself to the animals, so that first one sheep or bullock broke from the gate, and the rest followed. Unfortunately for this imaginative flight, the 'few stray straws' of John 2:15 are used in Acts 27:32 to tie up a boat.

One famous New Testament scholar insists that Mark's account of Christ's stilling of the storm was *not meant* to represent a nature miracle, but a psychological healing within the disciples' troubled hearts.

One of the finest exponents of the church's responsibility towards the under-privileged in society has pointed out how often the church has preferred, in her Bible-exposition, to follow her own doctrinal and ecclesiastical interests, hunting out proof-texts for dogmas, or studying in detail the tithing system in Israel for providing financial support for religion in society, or allegorising a remarkable story of social liberation, that of the exodus from Egypt, into a parable of the soul's eternal salvation. In all this she ignored, or explained away, the great moral and social protests of the prophets, the humanitarian spirit of the Jewish law, the compassion of Jesus towards the least and lowest. That is a most serious charge against the church's use of her own scriptures: but so often we find in the Bible only what we want to find.

Another serious historical example is the changing attitude of the early church towards military service, with its scriptural justification. Earlier Christian feeling about war was strongly pacifist: soldiers had to endure years of penance before taking Communion, for example. Much was made of Christ's saying that those who take the sword would perish by the sword; of his own refusal to ask for 'legions' of angels; of the kingdom's being 'not of this world', and the promises of peace from Isaiah to Jesus. God's commands to fight, recorded in Old Testament days, were set aside, either by cutting out of scripture everything Jewish (as Marcion did); or by relegating Old Testament teaching to 'an early stage' of revelation, or by allegorising the military stories into lessons on moral conflict (Origen).

But when Ambrose was faced by a professedly 'Christian' emperor asking for the church's support, and with 'heretics' fighting on the eastern frontiers, he went back to great soldier-examples like Joshua, Gideon, David, Judas Maccabeus, ignored Isaiah's promise of peace and appealed instead to Ezekiel's promise of 'victory' to the people of God, scarcely deigning to consider the New Testament teaching. It is easy to be cynical about such manipulation of scripture: we all do it.

If those who love the Bible can so mishandle it, what of those who 'twist' the scriptures 'to their own destruction' (2 Pet. 3:16)? Would any of us like our own daughters to copy Ruth's tactics in finding a husband? Can we accept the Old Testament system of concubinage into modern church life? or advise the saints to find comfort in old age as David did? Scripture was quoted persuasively in defence of the Inquisition, and of slavery, and in the relentless persecution of witches. It is still cited in vindication of apartheid, and of racialism; to justify support of the whole drugs and drink industry, with all its individual and social damage, because Jesus did one miracle with wine. And what spiritual distress, and distortion of the gospel, resulted from translating 'repentance' as 'penance'; and what confusion from describing Mary as 'full of grace' instead of simply as 'highly favoured'.

In a recent analysis of modern deviationist cults, seventeen-and-a-half pages on Jehovah's Witnesses quote scripture fifty-eight times. 'The Way International' claims to base its teaching wholly on the Bible — beginning with Paul: the Gospels are not

for Christians, but belong to the Old Testament.
Christian Scientists claim to build on 'The Teaching
of the Scriptures' interpreted by Mrs Mary Baker
Eddy's equally 'inspired' 'Key to the Scriptures'. The
Mormon sect offers 'an inspired translation' of the
Bible together with later documents of equal
authority revealed by angels to Joseph Smith. Some
of the stranger ideas of the Seventh Day Adventists,
concerning Christ's entry into the 'inner sanctuary'
in 1844, are likewise based upon 'scriptural
statements'. In some branches of the charismatic
movement, spiritual ecstasies and visions supersede
scriptural teaching; on the fly-leaf of one member's
Bible was written, 'I don't care what the Bible says,
I've had an experience.' And all the main Christian
denominations likewise, in spite of the variety of
their teaching, emphasis, worship and organisation,
firmly claim to be loyal to the same scriptures!

Faced with propagandists of all sorts of faiths,
many Christians will concede that 'Of course, you
can prove anything from the Bible'. That is another
retort which assumes the futility of appealing to
scripture in search for the truth. Such is the
confusion of mind and conscience into which biblical
interpretation has fallen.

The immeasurable loss of confidence and of
authority which this involves is hard to realise. At
one time, the appeal to scripture was powerful
enough to purify and reform the church, to discipline
wayward princes, to break up and refashion
Christendom, to kindle the Spiritual Awakening in
England and America, to initiate the world-wide
missionary movement, and to provide the platform
for vast evangelistic campaigns. Today, such an
appeal more often evokes cynical discussion and
spiritual division.

Faced with such confusion and dispute about the
value of the Bible in modern Christian life, what are
we to do? To abandon scripture, and turn to inner
voices and intuitions, to 'transcendental meditation'

that searches within one's own soul for light, or to philosophy of religion and an amalgam of all the world's rival faiths, in order to find truth and spiritual nourishment, would seem to any mature and intelligent Christian a quite desperate expedient. To those who through the years have tasted the good word of God, their faith and character and experience firmly built on the foundation of divine revelation, such suggestions are unthinkable. We have no alternative, but to go on insisting upon the supreme value and importance of scripture to any truly Christian life; and to wrestle faithfully and patiently with the task of finding sound and safe guidelines to assist us in discovering what scripture means to say.

Any doubt about the importance of scripture may for the Christian be resolved by considering the place of scripture in the experience and work of Jesus. From childhood, his mind was fashioned by the scriptures' teaching; in them he read his own mission and destiny as the servant-messiah; in echoes of the prophets he was addressed by God at his baptism, and with words of scripture he shrugged off the evil suggestions of the tempter. To his mind, men lived by every word of God.

In the synagogue at Nazareth, in controversy among crowds within the Temple courts, or talking with individuals, the sacred literature of his people was ever present to Jesus' mind. He cited and discussed it on all the issues of his day; he appealed to it in his own defence when accused of breaking the sabbath or desecrating the Temple. With its aid he explained to bewildered disciples the meaning of his own death. He declared that the Sadducees erred in their opinions because they did not know the scriptures properly, and blamed the Pharisees for reading the scriptures with minds prejudiced by tradition. And he died with the words of a psalm upon his lips.

Much of the public power of Jesus, and his appeal

to the common people, lay in his unanswerable use of their own scriptures to support his teaching, and in the illumination he brought to well-loved passages, until men commented that he spoke with authority and not as the scribes. The apostolic church, following his example, found the Old Testament scriptures a constant source of inspiration, illumination, instruction and rebuke, and a powerful aid to evangelism.

Such considerations leave no question of the place of scripture in Christian life and work, or of the value of right understanding of their use. Nevertheless Jesus knew that not all ways of appealing to scripture were equally profitable: he exercised considerable discrimination, and a royal freedom, in his own use of them — as we shall see.

We have then the highest authority, as well as the plainest need, for taking care in how we interpret the Bible. It needs effort as well as prayer, intelligence as well as sincerity. Martin Luther's 'last scribbled note' asserts that, as no one can understand Virgil who has not been a shepherd or a farmer for five years, and no one can understand Cicero who has not been a politician for twenty years, so 'nobody can understand the scriptures who has not looked after a congregation for one hundred years'. An exaggeration for the sake of emphasis: but the main point, that time, study, sharing with other minds, and putting truth into experience, are all necessary to the understanding of God's word, is simple truth.

But we must not exaggerate. We are to be concerned with establishing what the Bible *means*, which must involve questions of history, language, writing-methods, and the like. And to some extent that search for the scripture's precise meaning must underlie every use we make of God's word: but *not to the same degree*.

It is wise to use the great statements and invitations of scripture, rather than our own experience, as the basis of evangelism; but it would be pointless to enter into arguments with an unbeliever, or even with an enquirer, about the probable date of *Deuteronomy* or the historical truth of *Jonah*. The only issue that matters in such circumstances is what the hearer thinks about Jesus — until that is settled, no other biblical question has the least importance, or makes sense.

Nor is it necessary, in order to draw comfort, promise, and inspiration from a psalm to know all about its author and background. Neither need we understand all the historical circumstances and consequences in order to be moved to admiration or warning by the story of some biblical figure. Of course God may speak through his word to the humble in heart, for enrichment, rebuke or direction, without the reader requiring extensive knowledge of how the Bible came to be written, or the difficulties that beset translation. We must never consent to surrender scripture to the scholars, any more than to the priests and parsons.

It is when we proceed from that personal and pious use of scripture to lay down the doctrines of the Bible, to assert that what the Bible 'has said to our hearts' is what it actually *means*, and to require that others shall believe and behave accordingly, that we have need of far greater care and expertise, before we can assert that our 'interpretation' of scripture is 'the true one'. Even in our devotional reading, and in seeking for guidance, we can go sadly astray if we surrender to emotional and impulsive impressions of what the sacred words 'say' to us, in 'verses that positively glow with unearthly light', and 'leap out of the page'. Letting the Bible 'fall open' to give us guidance is again a wholly irreverent use of scripture, an appeal to the tightness of the stitching, rather than to the teaching of the Spirit. By such unthinking, unchecked occultism, Christians have been misled into disastrous excesses, into immorality, injustice to others, self-righteous pride and all uncharitableness, all defended on the ground that 'I felt that God's word said to me . . .'

The safeguard is self-understanding, humility of heart, willingness to consult more experienced Christians, and to grow in scriptural judgement by constantly increasing attention to sound principles of interpretation. Only so can our 'impression' of what the Bible says become an enduring and defensible conviction that this is what the Bible truly means.

To that end, the young Christian would do well to concentrate, not as so many seem to do on the 'spiritual meanings' of the Israelite Tabernacle or the intricate visions of *Revelation*, but on getting to know well the mind of Jesus. The convert should begin with *Mark*, reading right through at an evening's sitting, and then going through it again in sections of fifteen to twenty verses each day, thinking over each passage carefully. He should then do the same with *Luke*, then *John*, then *Matthew* and finally *Acts of the Apostles*.

In this way he will have begun to form a Christlike judgement with which to approach *Corinthians*, *Thessalonians*, *Philippians*, *Ephesians*, and then *Romans*, after which he may confidently go his own way in Old and New Testaments. To the end of his life he will continue to discover new treasure even in the most familiar fields of scripture, especially if he remains open to new light, information, and guidance. But not without labour. He must learn a Christlike discrimination in *all* he reads, a sense of the proportions of truth — what is central and what peripheral; he must distinguish carefully his convictions, proved in experience of God, from his opinions — mere summaries of what he knows at present; and he must gain insight and sound spiritual commonsense, if the Bible is to become to him 'an open book'.

By that time he will appreciate another remark of Martin Luther: 'No man sees an iota of the scriptures, but he that hath the Spirit of God.'

2

The Groundwork for Guidelines

The general principles of sound Bible study are not prescriptions for getting some predetermined meaning from the text: they arise directly from the way in which the Bible came to be written and preserved. The danger of any 'introduction', footnotes, or 'guides to interpretation' appended to the scriptures is that inevitably the reader is thereby 'conditioned' to find what he is told to find, and to miss all else. It is essential therefore to lay some solid foundation for whatever counsel is offered on 'How to read the Bible'.

A sacred book may be wholly divine, or wholly human but still inspiring, or a human book in which something more than human finds expression. The Koran is represented as the utterances of one man believed to be under the influence of direct divine inspiration, 'usually preceded by some sort of neurotic seizure in which his body began to tremble and beads of perspiration appeared on his forehead'. The Book of Mormon was discovered as a result of a vision of two angels directing Joseph Smith to its hiding-place: with it were supernatural pebbles (?lenses) by means of which it was read without being translated, and later also translated from an ancient 'Egyptian' script. Such is the story, though later visions communicated further divine revelations in similarly miraculous ways. The result in each case is a wholly supernatural book, totally given as to language, form, and meaning, every part equally ascribed to divine activity. The story of the Bible's production is not in the least like this.

Any good religious book, though a hymnbook is perhaps the best example, inspires pious thoughts, feelings, attitudes, and imparts comfort, guidance, instruction in the things of God. There is no question that the Bible is the most tested and the most powerful book of that kind, but no Christian would be content to say only that.

Christians assert (a) that the events recorded in the Bible (and much of it is simple historical record) are events in which divine purposes were fulfilled, in which the divine character was therefore made known, and which are thus the vehicles of God's self-revelation to man. The call of Abraham, the creation and redemption of Israel, the long story of her discipline, the coming of Christ and the creation of the church, are all divine acts which reveal God. The Bible therefore is the record of a long and shared divine revelation. The record of the events thus itself partakes of revelation and perpetuates it for succeeding generations, who by learning what God has done in past ages become aware of God's character and purpose for themselves.

(b) Further, a number of the actual writers who contribute to the Bible testify to personal divine inspiration as the source of their thought, insight and message. Such were Moses, in the giving of Israel's constitutional law; the poets who fashioned the thought and feeling of Judaist worship; the prophets who commented, protested and instructed on the issues of their day 'in the name of the Lord' because 'his Spirit' or 'his hand' came upon them; and apostles who counselled, instructed and warned young Christians and churches, having 'the mind of Christ'. The Gospel writers hid almost completely behind the inspiration of him whom they describe and the events they record. *Revelation*, too, is the work of a Christian prophet 'in the Spirit on the Lord's day' (1:9,10).

(c) It is integral to the Christian view of the Bible that all was shared, corporate, tested in the common religious experience of the people of God, from Abraham to the apostolic church. This is the Christian safeguard against individual fanaticism or frenzy, against the idiosyncrasy of the possessed or unbalanced visionary and the claims of the demagogue.

Throughout, the biblical revelation has all three notes of mental, moral and social health and sanity: the close relation to ongoing history and events taking place in the real world; the insights and inspiration of great and far-seeing personalities; and the constant sifting and confirmation by corporate religious experience, in which the revelation claimed to be from God is tested upon the conscience of the community.

Admittedly, the claim that such events, individuals, and corporate experience, together with the record itself, mediate a divinely given revelation is a declaration of faith, of which the truth cannot be demonstrated in any strictly logical and scientific way. It is a value-judgement passed upon the total contents of the Bible, plus the testimony of generations of Christians who have found that the Bible has brought them, not only increased knowledge of God, but the experience of his presence and grace. And it is wholly consistent with the attitude of Jesus towards the history and literature of his people. Acceptance of the divine origin of the Christian scripture is therefore no blind act of unsupported pious credulity, but a reasoned

assessment of a literature born out of the heart of the
events of which it tells, and conveying still the
meaning and power of those events to all who are
willing to receive.

But neither of these claims attempts to deny that
the book itself is nevertheless also a *human* book —
neither miraculously produced nor supernaturally
bestowed by inexplicable means, but the gathered
writings of men sharing the revealing events, the
inspiration, and the religious experience of the age in
which each lived.

*It cannot be said too often that the basic truth of
Christianity is incarnation* — the divine and eternal
enshrined, expressed and conveyed through the
earthly, the human, the temporary. The divine
Saviour and Son of God moved among men 'in the
form of a servant . . . in human form . . .' as the word
made flesh. The Spirit is present to our experience in
the lives of the ordinary Christians whom we meet
every day. The church, the Body of Christ, is known
to us only in the fallible and divided churches with
which we have to do. And the revelation that came to
man through Israel, in Christ, and by the Spirit, is
enshrined in a literature bearing all the marks of
law, poetry, history, folk-tale, songs, battle sagas,
proverbs, political comment, sermons, reminiscences, testimonies, correspondence, prophecies,
each stamped clearly with the writing style and the
living personality of its individual author.

Yet, through all that is so human, candid, heart-
moving in the Bible as a record of the fears, hopes,
disappointments, struggles and faith of generations,
through separate personalities, ages and
circumstances, there shines a timeless, increasing,
beyond-human truth and wisdom. Something is going
on which the writers neither invent nor control, but
which uses them. A divine treasure is carried in
earthen vessels, that the excellency of the power
might be seen to be of God and not of men.

This is where the *mode* of revelation affects the task of interpretation. Because the revelation of God has come through historical events and people, humanly recorded and described, sound interpretation distinguishes the human means from the divine content, in obvious but illuminating ways.

(i) The revelation comes in *human language*, indeed in *the* language of writer and readers of a given time and place, in Hebrew, Aramaic, some Persian, the Greek of everyday speech, and a little that is nearer to classical Greek. God just did not give the gospel in modern western tongues; if the message is to be shared by others not originally addressed, then the whole vexed problem of translation has to be faced, honestly and patiently.

Nor is it a question only of 'alien tongues'. As Luther quaintly remarks, complaining of the great difficulty of expressing divine things in human terms, 'we have only half-words and quarter-words'. In scripture, in addition, we have the characteristic eastern pictorial and poetic habit of speaking by analogies and allusions, rather than the western prosaic literalism. Precise definitions, scientifically accurate descriptions, of spiritual experience and moral causes and effects, are impossible, as with most things in which human motives, emotions, relationships and values are involved. Always the greater truth 'breaks through language and escapes'. It is foolish therefore to argue about the highly metaphorical language of the Bible as though it possessed scientific or legal exactitude. Holy men of God had to make do with the words and pictures that lay to their hands.

(ii) The revelation came through varied *human authors*, each with his own vocabulary, writing style, and forms of expression, each stamping his own individuality on his work. A passage from Isaiah hardly sounds like Moses or Malachi; we can all distinguish the psalms, proverbs or Paul from

Matthew, and Matthew from John. God spoke of old 'in many and varied ways', and the divine truth received a multifarious human accent.

Similarly, the revelation comes through all the normal variety of *human writing*. There is much of *history*, since the truth comes through experience: *Genesis, Kings,* the Gospels, *Acts* and much else must be studied as history, though with religious and evangelistic overtones. Sometimes the overtones almost dominate the story, as in *Judges* and *Chronicles*, where the history is told from a predetermined point of view to make a religious case. John's Gospel, too, is stated to be written for a theological purpose (20:30,31).

There is much again in the Bible of *poetry*, lyrical, liturgical, didactic, or simply the overflow of praise. Not the psalmists only, but the prophets and Jesus used the easily remembered poetic forms for a public unused to reading or taking notes. Prophetic writing consists largely of *comment* upon prevailing political and social conditions, as seen from God's throne — somewhat like the modern leading article in the more responsible newspapers, but analysing situations, exposing motives, offering counsel, warning of consequences, in the name of the Lord.

Legal and liturgical *statutes*, judgements, precepts, ordinances, occupy much of the earlier Old Testament. Moral teaching in the form of memorable *proverbs* comes later. In the New Testament, the *epistle* is developed as the vehicle of instruction, exhortation, and warning. And of course the Bible contains many *parables* — truth expressed in story form — a device known among the Greeks in Aesop, but more familiar in Jewish education and perfected by Jesus.

Thus the Bible embraces all the variety of human literature, expressing all the moods of the human heart. Even *humour* is not totally absent. Interpretation which ignores this variety of form cannot hope to pierce to the heart of any passage.

Suspicion is often aroused by the suggestion that perhaps a given chapter, or book, belongs not to one type of writing but to another. It cannot seriously be questioned that the book of Job is a *dialogue*, such as might be performed by speakers before an audience, a 'discussion programme' exploring serious points of view on the urgent question, 'Why does God permit suffering?' A prologue and an epilogue set the theme within the story of a particular individual, elsewhere referred to as a famous man of righteousness. This much seems beyond argument. But if we add, 'It does not need to be historical to make its point', then fierce controversy may follow!

So, too, the question whether the poetry of the *Song of Solomon* should be recognised frankly as Hebrew love-songs, and not a theological treatise on the relation of Christ to his church, written many years before Christ or his church appeared, divides Christians sharply. C H Spurgeon is said to have confessed that he did not know if 'Return, return, O Shulammite' was Christ calling to a backsliding church, or the old companions of the church calling her away from Christ, but 'to be sure of getting the truth, he preached on it quite earnestly first in one sense and then in the other'.

Is there any compelling reason why Jonah must be classed with biblical history, and not with biblical parables? Its message, its humour, remain unaffected by the decision. Granted that there are pitfalls to be avoided by the elimination of mere prejudice, the variety of material in the Bible must be acknowledged, and borne in mind, in the work of interpretation.

(iii) Because the revelation was given in concrete *human situations*, through successive personalities and historical experiences, it must at point after point be expressed in the terms current in successive periods, and applicable in the first instance to the

circumstances of those periods. This is crucial to all
sound interpretation, affecting the meaning of
scripture at many points. Yet all it is saying is that
when God spoke, he spoke to men, in their time, about
their needs, intending to be understood.

The plain fact that the Bible comprises sixty-six
separate books written over about a thousand years,
its story and teaching intimately interwoven with the
history of one people and its neighbours, culminating
in events crowded into little more than sixty years,
demands a historical approach. It is a matter of
demonstrable fact, rather than of belief or opinion,
that whatever word of God came to Israel or to the
church over such a span of time *was always related*
directly to the human situation addressed. Laws
were shaped to the daily life of the people expected
to live by them; prophets spoke to their
contemporaries about their politics, their ways, the
problems of their own times; the epistles, and even
the Gospels, were addressed to and shaped by the
needs of their original readers. The revelation was
always relevant, and that implies that it was always
relative. The historical circumstances and setting
provide always the first clue to the interpretation of
any passage.

Of course, God *could* have revealed himself in the
writings of one man at one point in time. But he did
not: he revealed himself through a long history.
Wilfully to ignore the setting in which each divine
word was first given, in order to find some far-
fetched, up-to-the-minute meaning, is to handle the
word of God deceitfully.

This truth of the historical context of revelation is
the fundamental principle of biblical interpretation,
though it is but the recognition of the process by
which God chose to make himself known. And it has
far-reaching consequences.

(a) It is hardly surprising that the word which God
sent through lawgiver, prophet, or saint to any

particular generation should be expressed within the scientific world-view of that generation — a flat earth, a three-tiered universe, demonology, ancient medical lore (as Isaiah's cake of figs recommended for a boil, mandrakes for infertility, wine for wounds). The general philosophic position of 'spiritism', for which all natural phenomena not otherwise explicable are ascribed directly to supernatural action by spirits of some sort, is likewise what we would expect in the earliest Bible books, without feeling bound thereby to accept that view for ourselves.

(b) Equally plainly, the divine revelation given in any age and relevant to its needs will find expression within the social climate and customs of that age, even though it may eventually stimulate protest and accomplish change. Slavery, concubinage, food and clothing tabus, multiple wives, harlotry are as much a part of the social milieu of the Old Testament as the flocks and herds of the early nomads, or the particular system of land tenure presupposed in ancient Israel.

Only within the social structure could the word be relevant to any given time and problem; but no Christian dogma requires that we adopt permanently any of the science, cosmology or customs in association with which the timeless truth was first disclosed. There is no difficulty, for most Christians, in making the obvious mental translations out of that time into ours, any more than in translating the New Testament message out of its Jewish and first century terms and customs into modern equivalents: but immense barriers are raised in the minds of modern readers when such adjustments are for reasons of dogma or of prejudice refused, and the distinction between the eternal truth and its historic dress is denied.

(c) The primary relevance of divine revelation to the age in which it was given implies also that

revelation develops as insight accumulates,
experience deepens, and man's capacity to receive is
matched by increasingly full divine disclosure. Jesus'
words, 'I have yet many things to say to you, but you
cannot bear them now' do not of course 'prove' this,
but they illustrate a principle that applies to all
revelation. His own setting of 'I say unto you' beside
what was said by them of old time, is also in line with
a developing revelation, and the whole New
Testament position rests on the conviction that a
former dispensation of promise, law, and partial
understanding has given place to a new age of
freedom, fulfilment, and further truth. Indeed, a
developmental view of revelation is already implied
in the Christian claim that Jesus is the fullest, the
ultimate, revelation of God.

(iv) The *human conditions*, needs and motivations
that helped to produce the scriptures are especially
discernible in the casual, almost accidental, origin of
the New Testament. Its authors had no thought of
writing for succeeding ages — the expected close of
the age with the return of Christ precluded any such
intention. The 'occasional correspondence' of
apostolic leaders, answering the churches'
questions, commenting upon reported developments,
conveying news, encouragement, greetings, counsel,
organising support, was only partially and slowly
preserved, copied and circulated. The writing of the
Gospels was the church's reaction to the passing of
the eye-witnesses of Jesus, and the rise of new
problems upon which his 'mind' was sought. Some
circulars or tracts, an apologetic treatise or two, an
underground pamphlet — all were produced to meet
immediate situations which must first be recalled
before any modern application of their teaching is
made.

It follows almost inevitably that no uniform
presentation of the Christian message is to be
expected in these documents. The New Testament

offers at least six approaches to the central
significance of Jesus: that shared by the first two
Gospels and *James*; those of John, of Paul, of Peter, of
Hebrews, and of the Gentile Luke. It is a serious
distortion of biblical teaching to force into artificial
uniformity the testimony of different writers
addressing different readers in different situations.
The teaching of the New Testament is consistent, but
not systematic; it is varied, and we must let each
writer put things in his own way, with his own
emphasis, and enjoy the diverse richness of thought
that results. 'For all things are yours,' as Paul told
the Corinthians concerning their rival teachers,
'whether Paul or Apollos of Cephas . . . all are yours;
and you are Christ's; and Christ is God's.'

Nevertheless not one of these writers, though
following his own style, sharing his own viewpoint
and facing his own situation, had any thought that he
was expressing his own ideas and no more. Each
spoke out of, and on behalf of, the central truth
committed to the church by Christ, each as he
believed the Spirit bade him speak. Paul indeed
draws a clear distinction between counsel for which
he can cite the direct authority of Jesus ('I have
received of the Lord . . .'), and counsel which he
himself is offering ('for the rest speak I, not the
Lord'): but even in that he believes that he has 'the
mind of Christ' and 'the Spirit of the Lord' to guide
his dictation (see 1 Cor. 11:23; 7:10,12; 2:16 and
7:40).

Thus in the New Testament as clearly as in the
Old, the mingling of divine authority with human
mediation is evident, and careful interpretation must
continually make allowance for the human factors
influencing the way in which the word of God was
given.

(v) The literature so accumulated by the church,
sifted and established as the spiritual judgement of
the church recognised and acknowledged its

inherent authority, had then to be *humanly copied*
over and over again through succeeding centuries.
For well over a thousand years the copying was done
by hand, on perishable and imperfect materials,
creating endless repeated possibilities of mistake,
and of error piled on error as copies were made of
already erring copies, and often of mistakes
imperfectly corrected. Even the invention of printing,
allowing production of thousands of facsimile copies
at one time, does not ensure accuracy — as any
newspaper reader knows. Who can imagine what
would happen if each copy of each daily paper were
made by hand?

Yet so the scriptures were handed down to us. The
result is that among the many 'witnesses' to what the
original words of the Bible were — some five
thousand manuscripts, whole or fragmentary,
worship-books, ancient translations, quotations in
the writings of the church Fathers, and the like — *no
two copies are exactly alike.* Over the sixty-six books
of the Bible, scores of thousands of variant readings,
slight or serious, have arisen. The claim sometimes
made, that the divine wisdom superintended the
preservation of the scriptures from all mischance
and error, must be tempered in its assurance by
some reference to the footnotes in any good Greek
Testament and in any competent English translation,
which warn the reader of places where the ancient
manuscripts disagree, or are obscure. *Every printed
copy* of the scriptures rests upon someone's choice
among the many alternative forms of text, someone's
decision that this or that word, or phrase, or
omission, most probably has the original writer's
authority.

After so many centuries of hand-copying, the
wonder is not that variations occur, but that so very
much of the text is confidently established.
Competent authorities assure us that the general
meaning, and the main truths, presented in the Bible

are nowhere rendered uncertain by textual variations: a study of the textual footnotes justifies that confidence. But on details, and in individual passages, there are no honest shortcuts to certainty.

We cannot now, in the face of what we know, close our eyes and say, 'Lord, I accept your word as authoritative, through and through, as it stands . . .' and pretend that the printer and the publisher between them have settled what the word of God should say. Nor can we honestly argue that the 'text received' in ignorance by the church, based on some twenty-five ancient copies, and nicknamed 'the received text' by a zealous publisher anxious for sales, 'is in fact the church's Bible in a way that the authors' text never was'. That attitude hardly merits examination: no one text ever was 'accepted by the church' — else we would have no problem. Moreover, that attitude makes the church (or the publisher) the arbiter of scripture, 'canonises' all the variations in a very few copies and arbitrarily discards all other copies as irrelevant. That is to make divine inspiration lie in the inaccuracies of careless scribes, perpetuated by tradition, and no longer in 'the holy men of God' who 'spoke as moved by the Holy Spirit'.

Of course, very few Bible readers can become competent judges of the evidence for this or that ancient version of a passage: but it is well to be aware that skilled and sincere scholars have pored over the manuscripts on our behalf, and to learn to take note when they warn us that here and there 'other ancient authorities' have some different text. A little humility is a great aid to interpretation!

(vi) That the Bible is, for the vast majority of its readers, a *humanly translated* book is so entirely taken for granted that its significance is usually overlooked. The story told of an early Puritan leader, John Smyth, exiled to Amsterdam for the sake of spiritual freedom, underlines the point. Smyth objected to the use of 'translated scriptures' in public worship as a 'formality': the original Greek and Hebrew were inspired, he said, but translations were subject to imperfection and error. A written translation was as much 'a human writing' as a prepared homily or a written prayer. The person leading worship should bring with him the Greek and Hebrew versions and translate on the spot by the help of the Spirit who first gave the word.

A somewhat impracticable position for today! But the reason alleged, that all translations are human productions, has a measure of truth that all interpreters must bear in mind. Every translation reflects something of the personal opinions, the background, and the individual taste of the translator. This is unavoidable. An exact equivalent in one language for what was written in another is impossible to find — for every language has its own nuances, overtones and accent. Translation is an art more than a science. Among the alternative English expressions which roughly represent what the Hebrew or the Greek words say, only the practice, skill, judgement and honesty of the translator can find the one nearest to the original thought. If he has misunderstood the author, missed the connection of thought, the nuances of words or the shades of emphasis, his translation will be inadequate, and might even mislead. And all the time his own religious opinions, experience and preferences will colour his judgement.

Examples will show how important this is to interpretation of God's word. Paul was fond of a particular expression (he uses it fourteen times) which came from the Hebrew for 'Away with such an idea', and which in Greek meant 'never let any such thing occur'. In current English we would say 'No! no! no!' or 'Never in this world', or 'Never let it be said', or perhaps 'No way!' The solemn translators of the King James Authorised Version, with due episcopal decorum, rendered it 'God forbid!' (Rom. 6:2 etc.). In the parable of the unjust steward, James Moffat used for 'steward' the regional-dialect word 'factor', betraying his own Scottish background.

Most copies of the Revised Standard Version have, for British readers, an American flavour, due in part to characteristic spelling (Savior, labor), but also to vocabulary. For the familiar English term for the Spirit, 'the Comforter', RSV uses 'the Counselor' (John 14:26, and with one 'l'!). This represents the Greek name, 'One called alongside to help', but in the purely legal sense of advocate, legal representative, rather than (as the Greek word permits) any friend, helper, priest, pastor, or even a good deed, which 'pleads one's cause'.

In 2 Timothy 4:6, an emotional passage, Paul says 'the time of my departure is at hand'. The word he uses gives us our word 'analysis', for its fundamental idea is of breaking up, or loosening. The word was used of loosening the moorings of a ship about to set sail on the open sea; of a soldier who 'having fought a good fight' had reached the age of demobilisation and peaceful retirement; of a traveller striking his tent and packing up his goods to resume his forward march: nothing of this imaginative range of suggestion is conveyed in Moffatt's bald translation, 'my time to go has come'.

Reproducing the author's thought is only part of the problem; the translator has to aim also at what experts call 'dynamic equivalence', a translation that will, so far as possible, make the same impact on the modern reader as the original did on the first readers. Literal and exact translation often 'leaves us cold' because the images and the emotive words of one language do not correspond with those of another. That is why modern translations seem often to avoid the beauty, rhythm and majesty that we desire in worship, and to aim for 'everyday language', 'vernacular' and 'slang' equivalents. The intention is, 'to let the plain unvarnished truth hit the ordinary reader straight between the eyes'. The result may not be elegant, but the attempt has this much excuse, that most of the New Testament was written in the plain, blunt speech of the market place.

This brief sketch of the human means by which the divine word was given deliberately excludes much that is of interest but would not materially affect interpretation. Before we can go on to ask what the Bible says to ourselves, we must first establish what the scriptures were originally intended to convey, and for this such knowledge of the background and process of revelation is quite essential — as well as richly rewarding. It is only upon such understanding of the Bible's own story that guidelines for sound interpretation can safely be based.

3

Resulting General Guidelines

The greatest hindrance to sound biblical interpretation is the assumption that any individual's 'feeling' about a passage, his 'spiritual intuition', or (what is worse) some private divine revelation, settles for him, and should settle for everyone to whom he speaks, what that passage means. It is hard for some Christians to accept that liking or not liking a particular interpretation, liking or not liking the speaker who maintains it, is totally irrelevant.

It is essential to have grounds for your view of any scripture, if it is to be defensible at all, and if others are to be persuaded of it. This is not to set reason above scripture, but above individual fancies about the scripture. Yet how often, after careful discussion of the grounds for alternative interpretations, one is met with the stubborn reply 'I do not care what you say, I have always understood it my way, and I shall go on doing so!'

Acceptable reasons for any interpretation will rest, first, on the actual meaning of the words used by the writer or speaker; that may involve the use of dictionaries, and also noting how such words were used at that time and by such authors. They will rest, secondly, on what the original readers would understand by the words, given their situation and their need. And thirdly, acceptable reasons would rest on how the resulting interpretation harmonises with what that writer, or others of his circle, is known to have thought and taught in similar circumstances.

Expressed so briefly, this sounds complicated and vague: it must be spelled out. But let it first be repeated that the only alternative to such a reasoned approach is the purely subjective, instinctive, emotional one, which claims to discern 'what the passage says' by some inner light, sometimes mistaken for spiritual insight, but actually nothing more than an individual's preference for certain pet ideas which he professes to find everywhere in scripture.

Six centuries ago the reformer-evangelist John Wycliffe, 'the morning star of the reformation', sent out through English towns and villages his travelling preachers, some of them insufficiently trained. His advice to them is still worth quoting: 'It shall greatly help ye to understande scripture if thou marke not only what is writ or spoken, but of whom, and to whom, with what words, at what time, where, and to what intent, with what circumstances, considering what goeth before, and what followeth.' That is still the high road to sound interpretation: but with today's added knowledge, and in today's climate, it has to be amplified and defended. Our guidelines are six.

(1) Today, one must begin with the counsel to *choose your version of the scriptures very carefully.* It is helpful, and interesting, to have two or three translations at hand to consult and compare: but the serious Bible reader will have one version for constant study and seek to get to know it thoroughly.

Though the eloquence, majesty, and warmth of the King James Authorised Version place it in a class by itself in the affection of many Christians, its archaic language, and the obscurity of its many overlong sentences, are serious disadvantages. But more serious is its very slender textual basis, in that 'Received Text' which (as we saw) was supported by only twenty-five conveniently available ancient authorities out of the five thousand or so now available. Generations of fine Christians nourished their spiritual lives on the result without coming to noticeable harm: but that is no reason for continuing to confine the scripture to so haphazard a text.

Current 'revisions' of the King James Authorised Version which do not extend to a thorough and competent revision of the text used, must share the same inadequacy. The earnest Bible reader will seek, in the introduction to any version which he plans to buy, some definite assurance — more than the publisher's evasive generalities — that due attention has been given to recent competent attempts to recover the original words of scripture. He will seek also a version that by its footnotes will keep him fairly informed of the more important variant readings in the ancient manuscripts — as the Revised Standard Version, and the New English Bible, for examples, seek to do. He will not find the great majority of variants very disturbing, but he will want to be aware of them.

The earnest reader will also bear in mind the human factors that influence every translation, the private opinions and idiosyncrasies of translators, and the widely different purposes and audiences for which varying translations are made. He will in consequence choose a translation made by a group of representative scholars of varying 'schools' and backgrounds, whose individual preferences may be expected to cancel each other out in the long discussions and majority decisions that prepare the translation, and so yield an unbiassed result.

The wise Christian will reject very firmly *all* versions of the Bible that have a particular propaganda-line to defend, whether the 'New World Translation' of the Jehovah's Witnesses, the 'One Man's View' translations that aim to make money by stressing 'originality'; the avowedly Roman Catholic version, or the much-advertised 'evangelical version'. All such are propaganda, sadly misplaced, emphasising where they should minimise the prejudices of translators. There is nothing at all, in any theological bias or in personal piety, to guarantee competence in Greek grammar, or skill in judicious translation.

Two seductive temptations call for especial vigilance. One is, to settle at once for the simplest, easiest-to-read version and leave it at that. The Bible has profound things to say, and some of the problems it wrestles with cannot be discussed in words of one syllable at a child's level of understanding. The heart of the message is childlike: but on many aspects of the Bible's teaching, simplicity is purchased only at the cost of superficiality.

The other temptation is to juggle with the many available translations in order to 'justify' the meaning we want to find, and even to preach on texts taken in varied translations in turn to urge 'what the text might be made to mean'. The last-named habit is ingenious, sometimes, but essentially lazy, and certainly not 'the ministry of the word'.

Expanded versions and paraphrases which do not pretend to accurate translation, but set out to rewrite the original in more elaborate form, are really running commentaries, useful as such. The attractiveness of the New English Bible lies here — and its weakness: as one authority on translations says, 'its manifest concern to avoid at all costs any trace of literalism in its renderings' makes it a far less satisfactory basis than the Revised Version or the Revised Standard Version for serious study of the Bible. Like all explanatory footnotes, paraphrases should be read carefully, even critically, and with constant reference to accurate translations, to check whether the author's personal opinions are valid.

(2) The earnest Christian will train himself to *read what is there*. No general guideline for Bible reading is more rewarding than this, or more surprising. For random examples, out of many —

Paul nowhere tells wives to obey their husbands; he does use the word of children obeying their parents, and the traditional marriage vow seems to have transferred it to wives.

Luke does not say that Jesus in Gethsemane 'sweat great drops of blood'.

The Bible nowhere says that money is the root of all evil, or that God tempers the wind to the shorn lamb.

Nor does scripture anywhere require that women should wear hats in church: Paul does discuss the propriety of a woman's wearing of a veil, probably a sort of yashmak.

The Bible says plainly that the great heroes of faith all died without receiving what had been promised them.

Genesis never mentions Satan's presence in Eden: in fact, the devil is not mentioned in scripture earlier than the book of Job.

Nor does the Bible ever describe Satan as an angel who for pride was cast out of heaven; in *Job* he is an official of the heavenly court.

The lovely promise, 'I will give thee the treasures of darkness' was not given to a Christian, or to a godly Jew, but to a pagan.

The Gospels declare plainly that at Nazareth Jesus *could* do no mighty work; that he was weary with journeying; that he did not know the time of his second coming; that he constantly asked questions; and that he was tempted. An epistle adds, 'tempted *in all points* as we are'; that he learned obedience by what he suffered; and that he was *made* perfect through suffering.

Christian baptism is never in the New Testament described as a confession of faith, though it is associated with the confession of sins.

The twenty-third psalm is not 'the shepherd psalm': sheep do not lean on the 'shepherd's' staff, nor sit at table, their heads anointed and their cups full.

Jesus did say, according to Matthew, 'Blessed are you, Simon Bar-Jona! ... I tell you, you are Peter (*Petros*) and on this rock (*petra*) I will build my church ...'

Jesus also said, according to John, 'If you forgive the sins of any, they are forgiven; if you retain the sins of any, they are retained.'

Paul never says that the present human body will be raised again: he expressly argues that it will be vastly changed — 'What you sow is not the body which is to be ...'

The New Testament nowhere declares, simply and without addition, that Jesus is God: always it says 'Son of God', 'God manifest in the flesh', 'image of God', 'bearing the very stamp of God's nature', 'God was in Christ', 'the word was God and was made flesh', but never the unqualified 'Jesus is God' (Denney, but see Rom. 9:5 RSV margin).

The New Testament says very clearly that in every nation any one who fears God and does what is right is acceptable to him.

To all such surprising statements, many eager Bible readers would add, quite automatically, 'Ah, but ...' If the first rule of sound interpretation is to choose a reliable version, the second is certainly to *break that habit* of bending what we read into conformity to some preconceived opinion. Learn to read what is there without the distorting spectacles of traditional interpretation, childhood conditioning, or any other unthinking assumption about 'what the writer meant', or 'meant to say', or what some other writer in some other book has to say. There may well be a balancing truth elsewhere to take into account: but the automatic 'correction' of a surprising passage to force it into line with what we already believe, merely blinds us to truth.

This guideline has greater importance than might appear, and it has the Master's authority. For it enshrines that warning he uttered about making void the word of God through our tradition (Mark 7:13). The Pharisees and scribes were confident they knew 'what the law demanded', and they possessed great skill in making every passage yield a meaning which supported their view. Traditional piety certainly required that a man should not swear falsely, but perform to the Lord whatever he had sworn (Matt. 5:33). If therefore in spitefulness or in temper a man swore *at* his parents, declaring they should never again have a penny from him, but that he would give all he earned to God first, and used the sacred vow-formula 'korban' — then however much he regretted it when he cooled down, his vow was binding. That was the rule of the sacred Torah.

And so, said Jesus, you no longer permit him to do anything for his father and mother — although the word of God requires that a man honour and support his parents at all times! Your tradition 'empties' God's word of all authority: and traditional assumptions that we know what God will say before we read his word always does make the reading 'void'. Their 'tradition' was legalist, ours is usually evangelical, *but the effect is the same*. The plainest text cannot get its message through to us, because we learned long ago how to explain away its awkwardness, how to harmonise it with the fixed and predetermined view of the gospel which we were taught. We can no longer read or hear any passage except in the already established connection in our minds; its true meaning is inaudible amid the echoes of those who first taught us what we ought to find in scripture.

The Bible can become a fresh book to hearts that determine, against all difficulties, to read it 'as if for the first time', pondering the most familiar words, paying alert attention to precisely what it says.

(3) *Always pay attention to the contexts — all three of them.* The oddest of all attitudes towards the Bible is that which treats it as something between a *Dictionary of Religious Quotations* and a *Spiritual Family Doctor.* On the one hand, it comprises a large anthology of wise, perceptive or beautiful passages on the general theme of religion; one need not trouble overmuch where they came from, but just study or enjoy them as they occur. On the other hand, spiritual wisdom consists in knowing where to look up the best prescription for this or that spiritual ailment: copies exist in which directions for finding the prescriptions most often needed are printed inside the cover!

This strange way of handling the Bible as a collection of isolated paragraphs, sentences, stories, each one of which is to be considered on its own, is fostered by the familiar framework of chapters and numbered verses; by some systems of Daily Bible Readings, which apportion widely separated 'bits' of scripture to successive days and leave to the reader the absorbing game of finding some connection; by the slavish habit of some preachers who 'take' a text for whatever they plan to say, however remote or irrelevant it might be. Even the teaching of memory-texts to children encourages this misunderstanding, unless some intelligence in selection and explanation is exercised. The attitude is also related to the curious idea, widespread among Christians, that one does not read a Bible book straight through — it just is not done!

(i) We shall not get far in biblical interpretation until we learn to ignore the verse breaks and the chapter breaks altogether. For fifteen hundred years the church managed without our present system. It was introduced in the early sixteenth century by Stephanus, and the story is told that he did the work while jouneying on horseback. True or not, the picture conjured up would explain much — a quill pen held above the manuscript and the jogging of the horse causing marks at random places, breaking the books into disjointed fragments! One chapter ends in a comma; often the sense of a chapter runs over into the next without a break; and sometimes the whole connection of thought is destroyed because for no apparent reason a verse or chapter breaks off abruptly. The idea of numbering the margins for easy finding of a paragraph was a good one: the way it was done has been a tragedy for intelligent reading.

We have to teach ourselves over again to see each sentence as part of a paragraph, each paragraph as part of a story or argument or message, and the whole drift of the writing as a single book, poem, letter or history. We need not, of course, always begin at the beginning, but we must never forget that the writer did so. The meaning of each sentence depends on what led up to it and what follows: to tear it from where the author placed it is to lose the key to its purpose and distort its sense. This is observing *the literary context*.

If this counsel seems over strict, consider what the Bible may be charged — and quite truthfully — with saying, if the literary context is ignored:

Scripture says, 'There is no God' (Ps. 14:1).

Scripture says, 'You are gods' (Ps. 82:6; compare John 10:34).

Scripture says, 'Let us eat and drink, for tomorrow we die' (1 Cor. 15:32).

Scripture says, 'Let the evildoer still do evil, and the filthy still be filthy' (Rev. 22:11).

Scripture says of Jesus, 'Who is this that speaks blasphemies?' and 'He is possessed by Beelzebul, and by the prince of demons he casts out the demons' (Luke 5:21; Mark 3:22).

But such examples are abundant, of Bible texts that utter misleading nonsense when torn from their original context.

(ii) *The historical context* is equally important. For examples: it is impossible to reconcile Isaiah's assurance that Jerusalem would remain unspoiled with Jeremiah's repeated warnings that the city was doomed, unless the changing historical situation be understood. Nor, without considering the background, can we harmonise the psalmist's celebration of the glories of the house of God, which he loves, with the scorn of Jeremiah towards those who continually cry 'The temple of the Lord, the temple of the Lord, the temple of the Lord', or with the anguished plea of Malachi that someone would shut the temple doors and have done with it.

Without understanding the historical circumstances, we cannot see how Paul can plead for Christians' support, prayers and taxes for 'the powers that be' (the pagan government of Rome), which are ordained of God to defend those who do right, while Peter can warn Christians that they may well do good and yet suffer for it, and *Revelation* summon to rejoicing over the downfall of the world power as the evil agent of Satan. Paul in 1 Corinthians advises Christians against entering upon marriage, but the Pastoral Epistles advise younger women to marry and bear children — so far have the circumstances and the church's expectation changed meanwhile.

It is exceedingly difficult to understand the problem that arose for Paul, at Corinth only, over the gifts of the Spirit, or his somewhat uncertain attitude about it, until one remembers that Corinth was a city of pagan shrines at which every one of the gifts claimed for the Spirit of Jesus — healing, tongues-speaking, interpretation of tongues, wisdom, knowledge, prophecy — were loudly claimed by the devotees of heathen deities. The Corinthian

Christians desired to make equally loudly rival claims for their own faith — and Paul will not suppress their zeal or deny their richness of gifts, but he does desire to woo them to seek the more excellent way of wisdom and love.

Hundreds of examples could be given where the simple citation of scripture texts without reference to their date and the circumstances that evoked them makes for total confusion. If there is one absolutely fundamental rule for biblical interpretation it is this: *Every passage means what the original writer intended it to say to the people he intended it to help.* This follows inexorably from the historical relevance which we saw to be characteristic of God's revelation of himself to men, always in direct relation to their situation, understanding and need, and in language and form intelligible to those addressed. Any 'application', or secondary meaning, later interpretation, 'prophetic overtone' or 'hidden significance' found in a passage may be imaginative, logical, ingenious, spiritually valid, fanciful or plain piffle: it will always be the opinion of the interpreter and not the meaning the writer intended. And what the writer intended determines the meaning, every time.

To discover that meaning we must learn all we can about the writer himself, his situation and purpose, about the readers, their circumstances and their need, and what the language used would convey at that time to such writer and readers. An illuminating example is the beautiful and forceful little epistle, *1 John.* To note carefully that certain former Christian teachers have 'gone out' of the writer's circle, drawing others after them (2:18,19; 4:1-6; compare 1:3); and to piece together from the epistle the teaching about Christ and Christian morals which these schismatics were propagating, is to possess at once the clue to what the writer intends to say, and why.

He himself stands with those who 'from the
beginning' saw and heard and touched the eternal
life manifested in Christ, and who heard the original
commandments of the Lord concerning Christian
behaviour. He addresses those now tempted to
wander after new teaching, which appears to be an
intellectual version of Christian faith but actually
destroys the heart of the gospel by denying for
philosophic reasons the incarnation of Christ in the
flesh; and which apparently offers a higher, mystical
liberation from elementary Christian morality but
actually subverts the hearers into sin and
lovelessness. The writer pleads that they will remain
within the apostolic fellowship, hold fast to the
original message, test carefully all claims to higher
spirituality, and keep themselves from shams. He
defines, analyses, warns, with utmost clarity: yet he
never accuses or blames a single person, or forces an
opponent on to the defensive.

Verse after verse lights up with this historical
approach, and with an appreciation of the danger of
this 'gnostic' heresy on both the theological and the
ethical fronts. Without it, the epistle seems to be a
mere rambling reverie.

When such information about the historical
background and context of a passage is not available
because date or authorship are unknown, our
interpretation can be only tentative and cautious,
and may be reduced to nothing more than 'what the
passage now says to me'. The twenty-third psalm, for
example, is certainly a Jewish religious lyric of great
beauty and depth, testifying to what a Hebrew saint
had found in God. Traditionally it is attributed to
David; the present heading to the psalm shows that
at least it belonged to the collection known as
David's. If the final verse be translated 'I shall dwell
in the house of the Lord for ever', such a hope of
immortality, compared with other biblical passages,
suggests a period later than David's; if we note the

Hebrew, 'for length of days', and the alternative marginal translation 'as long as I live', then the psalm's date could well be earlier. Certainty is impossible. Nothing in the psalm can refer directly to Jesus; it is written of 'Yahweh', though Christians may think that its inner truth shines still more clearly since Jesus came: that God is indeed a faithful shepherd, a trustworthy guide, and a bounteous host to those who trust in him.

One less welcome consequence of the close relation of revelation to its historical setting is that we must be careful about asking the Bible's answers to the urgent, complex problems which modern life poses. We long for a clear word of the Lord on many of today's moral issues: but our problems had not arisen when scripture was penned — artificial contraception, surgical abortion, heart and other organ transplanting, genetic engineering, nuclear war, the conservation of earth's resources, the desperate hunger of millions of people. To ask the Bible our questions in our modern terms must distort the meaning of scripture considerably: the questions must at least be reworded into scripture's terms, before we can hope for scriptural replies. This does not by any means make the appeal to scripture useless, but it cautions us against the slick citation of texts which originally had no relevance to the problems we relate them to.

We shall return to this vital question of the relevance of scripture to modern questions: but already we can say that the strictly historical approach to scripture does illumine the ways of God with men, and of men with each other; it does yield abiding principles of moral and social behaviour which experience has proved beneficial and the human conscience has approved; and it does set before us the supreme example and spirit of the Lord Jesus Christ, defined and explored in the New Testament. We have therefore more than isolated

pronouncements made in another age, from which to
'extrapolate' — draw out and apply to new
situations — the guidance we so sorely need. But the
historical context remains the determinative clue to
what the Bible itself is saying.

(iii) The third context to be observed is *the biblical
context* — the relation of each passage to the
message of the Bible as a whole. This requires the
kind of scriptural wisdom, observing 'the proportion
of truth', which only some years of sincere Bible
study can develop. It would obviously be wrong to lay
down as a Christian rule governing personal
relationships, 'The Bible says, an eye for an eye and
a tooth for a tooth'. So it does, but the Bible, and
indeed the Lord of the Bible, say explicitly that this
early precept will no longer do — 'I say to you . . . if
any one strikes you on the right cheek, turn to him the
other also . . .'

This contrast provides a fair example of
development within scripture. The Mosaic rule was
itself a distinct advance upon the unlimited revenge
for even small injuries which less civilised levels of
society condoned; Moses limited retaliation to a just
equivalent of the injury suffered: 'only' an eye for an
eye, a tooth for a tooth. With that limitation,
savagery ends and civilisation begins. Jesus however
moves forward to the standard expected in the
kingdom of God: no retaliation at all, but good
returned for evil, and love shown even towards
enemies. It takes the whole Bible to expound the
'biblical' truth.

The mass execution of a family for the father's
plundering of captured Jericho is not the Bible's last
word on corporate responsibility. This story,
together with the warning that God visits the sins of
the fathers upon the children to the third and fourth
generation, must be read along with Ezekiel's reply
to the people's complaint about God's unfairness —
'The fathers have eaten sour grapes and the

children's teeth are set on edge'. Ezekiel declares plainly that in future Israel shall not be able to say this; 'the soul that sinneth it' — and it alone — 'shall die'. The 'proportion of truth' emerges when the corporate consequences of sin and individual guilt are considered together: taken alone, either statement would be a half-truth, and not 'what the Bible says'.

Even Jesus' instruction to the Twelve not to take their mission to the Gentiles but only to 'the lost sheep of the house of Israel', and his own reply to the Syro-Phoenician 'It is not fair to take the children's bread and throw it to the dogs', are not the last word of scripture on inter-racial evangelism. The later words of Jesus himself, beside the story in *Acts* and the mission and letters of Paul, leave no doubt that the gospel is for all men.

Because divine revelation clarifies with man's growing experience, and develops with man's capacity to understand, it is the total unfolding story that yields the final truth, and not any formulation of words at an intermediate stage. Always, the 'many and various ways' of revelation in the past (Heb. 1:1) must give place to what God now says through one who is 'a son'. The divine word is mediated through history: but through the whole history, and in due historical perspective: that is why the citation of isolated texts irrespective of their historical and biblical context can be so misleading.

(4) *Respect faithfully the imaginative language* of eastern writing, so very characteristic of scripture. What are western literalist and logical minds to make of God's strong hand and outstretched arm, his eyes, ears, nostrils, his 'repenting', his 'grief of heart', his 'smelling a pleasing smell' of burning animals, his saying in his heart that he would never again curse the ground? How are we to explain to young people God the leader of armies ('Lord of hosts'), the lion, the strong tower, the father, the

husband, the potter, the shepherd, the consuming fire, and all the rest? Or God the sculptor, shaping the wet clay with his fingers to the image of a man and then breathing life into its clay nostrils to make — a man!

All such talk, easy and familiar to Bible-lovers, sounds incredible to new readers with no Christian background. The real difficulties arise when established Christians, who take the figurative language in their stride, bridle with suspicion and resentment if anyone suggests that other Bible expressions are also figurative, imaginative, suggesting and picturing truth in the eastern fashion, but not defining it precisely, in a western way.

It troubles no one that Jesus, who was a carpenter, calls himself a shepherd, or even a door — until some ingenious preacher begins to explain that the latch is conscience, and the hinges are the church and the gospel (or Catholic and Protestant, or the Old and the New Testament, or any other pair of items remotely religious that takes his fancy). Such an example irritates by its silliness: but let someone try to draw out the figurative meaning of 'This is my body' — and see what troubles arise!

In a world where the holding of individuals for ransom, whether prisoners of war, kidnapped travellers, or slaves, was commonplace, the biblical notion of 'redemption' — buying another's freedom by the payment of a ransom — was a metaphor ready to hand. It well describes God's deliverance of Israel from Egypt into the freedom of Canaan, and Christ's deliverance of sinners whose life and freedom were justly forfeit, by dying for them ('The Son of man came . . . to give his life as a ransom for many'). The meaning is clear, the metaphor vivid, the truth moves the heart to gratitude like that of liberated slaves; and the whole idea gained added weight from the practice of showing public benevolence, or gratitude to a pagan god, by buying a slave into freedom in the name of the god, to whom henceforth the slave would 'belong'. Paul makes great use of this idea of belonging to the Christ who bought us at the price of his own life, to set us free.

The prosaic minds of literalist theologians, however, refuse to treat the New Testament language as an inspired attempt to express the inexpressible in a figure of speech. They reduce the glowing metaphor to a precise definition, and argue about the amount of the ransom, to whom it was paid, and whether, since Jesus rose again, it was ever paid in the end! So with the other great attempts to say what Jesus' death meant for the apostolic believers — acquittal after being found guilty (a legal metaphor, 'justification'); removal of causes of ill-will and restoration of peace (a political metaphor, 'reconciliation'); forgiveness of debt (a commercial metaphor); the domestic figure of a Servant of the Lord doing for men what they could not do for themselves; the defeat of the Prince of this world and triumph over the powers of evil (a military metaphor); the offering of atoning sacrifice, human not animal (a priestly metaphor).

These are the great traditional terms to express the meaning of Christ's death, so far unsurpassed. But the radiant images fade and die in literalist minds which argue doctrines out of poetry and theologise adoring love. The metaphors become doubled, trebled, and confused: washing away defilement and atoning blood become 'washed in blood' (once even the New Testament speaks so); and the blood in Jesus' veins is piped into a fountain in whose basin sinners are 'plunged'. If we would use imaginative language more imaginatively, we would read more carefully, and feel much more deeply, the glorious biblical truths that the scriptural pictures vividly represent for us, but which we pedestrian westerners only argue about.

(5) *Handle all symbolism with especial care.* Not

mental images alone, but symbolic persons, events and places fill the Bible's pages. From the talking serpent in Eden to the city with gates of pearl and streets of gold; from the brazen serpent in the wilderness to the four horsemen of the apocalypse; from prophets wearing iron yokes or breaking inscribed tiles, to the bread on the Table of the Lord, the tearing of the temple veil at Christ's death, and the tongues of fire at Pentecost, scripture offers endless opportunities for 'allegorising', 'spiritualising', and the ingenious decoding of hidden meanings.

The whole story of the Exodus of Israel from Egypt to Canaan, in all its details, becomes a parable of Christian life. In John's Gospel Christ is the ladder of Jacob's dream, the healing serpent on a pole, the lamb that takes away sin, the pillar of fire and water from the rock of the wilderness journey; the healing of the paralysed demonstrates Christ's life-giving word, the cure of blindness shows him to be the light of the world, the feet-washing symbolises Christ's cleansing power, the water and the blood from Christ's side represent (presumably!) baptism and the Lord's supper.

Biblical symbolism has obviously to be reckoned with, but two dangers are obvious. There are real difficulties in the story of the raising of Lazarus: they can be resolved if we take the story as a fine dramatic *symbol* of the truth that Jesus is the resurrection and the life — and not a real event at all. Questions are raised about the story of Joseph's supposed rise to fame in Egypt — but then, Joseph is really just a type of Christ! Naaman and his leprosy have been almost 'spiritualised' out of Old Testament history into illustrations for evangelistic sermons. Isaac, Moses, Joshua, David, Aaron and his garments, the tabernacle in the wilderness and its furniture and a hundred other details of God's dealing with Israel, have all at times been 'allegorised' into the thin air of types, foregleams, prefigurings and anticipations of Christ and his story. A famous modern scholar has argued that Joshua circumcised Israel before they crossed the Jordan to show that confirmation should precede baptism in Christian experience! And hundreds of Easter sermons have suggested that the 'real message' of the resurrection-story is that truth, beauty and goodness are indestructible — the story symbolises a philosophic truth.

The most dangerous of all the heresies that assailed the infant church was gnosticism, which claimed to possess a higher, exclusive, more spiritual understanding of the gospel story, such as only the more intellectual and 'spiritually minded' could grasp. Gnostics held that that the accounts of Jesus' birth, life, death and resurrection were just the ABC of divine truth, told in symbolic language for those unable to comprehend the lofty philosophic truth about God and eternal life. All the salvation-history of the incarnate and dying Lord they relegated to the status of 'parables' of spiritual philosophy — symbols of great ideas, not actual events. Those who 'spiritualise' Bible history into types, allegories and symbols of evangelical truths are perpetuating the gnostic heresy.

The second danger is that of carrying this line of interpretation to inordinate lengths. A sermon on the seamless robe of Christ dwelt first on Mary's love in weaving this garment for Jesus, and then on the unity of the 'seamless' church, which men must not tear asunder. A neat argument for making Mary the mother of the church! It is said there are one hundred and fifty-three different 'explanations' of the one hundred and fifty-three fish caught by the disciples in John 21 — beside the obvious one, that fishermen always count their catch. Yet none of this is more fantastic than the sermon which added the oil of the Spirit to the fires of Pentecost and the water of baptism to make the (steam) power of the Spirit.

Some restraining principles are obviously needed
in dealing with scripture's symbolism. (a) An
editorial note in Augustine's *Confessions* says 'We
have no right to turn historical facts into allegories
unless they were designed to be so' — as the
sacrificial system of Israel was *both* effective in its
time *and* a promise of perfect atonement to come. (b)
It is safer never to add to the symbols explicitly
given. When Paul wrestles with hidden meanings in
Hagar and Jerusalem, saying 'This is an allegory', we
are justified in wrestling with him, if we can. When
John says of the feet-washing that the disciples
understood it only afterwards, then we are warned
of more meaning than is immediately apparent. But
that does not give us license to claim occult meanings
in the five porches of Bethzatha, the five husbands of
the Samaritan, in the cloak Paul left with Carpus
('fruit'), or the three or four miles the disciples rowed
without Jesus. The *given* symbols should suffice.

(c) Discrimination, a sense of truth, and good taste
are needed too. The rending of the temple veil as
Jesus died is obviously mentioned for some purpose;
its meaning not being explained, our interpretation
should be tentative, not dogmatic. That it was night
when Judas chose to go out of the presence of Christ
suggests a spiritual truth — but no more. That
Isaac's servant, sent to find a bride for his master,
provides a pleasant basis for a sermon on the wooing
ministry of the Spirit, numerous preachers could
testify: but where does such manipulation of
scripture end? And if evangelicals may do it, why not
Mormons?

Some spiritualising is harmless, some is silly, some
is tampering with God's word. We must not confuse
ingenuity with inspiration. We may sometimes
illustrate a truth by a parabolic incident (as we might
illustrate Christ's reigning through suffering by a
reference to the *crown* of *thorns*): but we must not

base truth upon illustrations, nor pretend that the illustration proves the point. And when we exercise our fancy upon Bible incidents, characters and statements, we must remember that we are giving the same freedom to other Christians, and to the cultists, to exercise their fancy also — leaving ourselves no ground on which to refute them. One man's ingenious spiritualising is no more authoritative than another's.

(6) *Read ever with open mind, listening heart, and ready will.* We have already promised to return to the question of the relation of the Bible to modern questions, which will take us somewhat beyond interpretation into application. But even as a guideline to sound *interpretation*, it is necessary to stress that what we are reading in scripture is moral and spiritual truth, a word of God intended to reveal him still to those who read it. On the one hand, we shall certainly miss what the Bible is saying if we seek only for ammunition against controversialists, or if we seek 'evidence' on scientific theories, or proof-texts supporting what we are determined to believe, or justification for our chosen life-style, or 'Women's Lib', or our denominational position.

On the other hand, divine truth is ever personalised: God speaks, not to satisfy our curiosity but to guide our feet, and a devout watchfulness for 'what God the Lord would say' is essential to scriptural insight. With all our care to observe the sound guidelines of linguistic and historical study, we shall still gain little profit unless now and again an unforeseen illumination of mind or conscience reveals an ideal, a truth, an opportunity, a duty, that we have not previously glimpsed, *and we go and do something about it.* Unless in this way, our care for right interpretation leads on to new spiritual experience, larger vision of God's will, we may find the scripture increasingly silent and remote.

One thing is sure: such experiences of the kindling,

awakening, nourishing, illuminating and directing power of God's word make all the labour of careful interpretation immensely worthwhile.

4

Guidelines for the Old Testament

It is startling to recall that the apostolic church lived and prospered without a scripture of its own. Christianity began as a bookless religion, dependent on the example of older Christians for the instruction of converts ('What you have learned and received and heard and seen in me, do . . .' Phil. 4:9); and borrowing the scriptures of another, hostile faith for its textbook. It was many generations before the new faith possessed an authorised Testament of its own.

Since Christianity began as a sect within Judaism, proclaiming Jesus as the fulfilment of Old Testament faith and hope, the adoption of the Old Testament was historically inevitable, though it brought some disadvantages as well as benefits. And it must be admitted that Christian interpretation of the Old Testament was often unorthodox, discovering ideas like virgin birth, a suffering Servant of the Lord, the Messiah as 'Branch' = nezer = Nazarene, and even the Trinity, where no Jewish scholar would find them.

We may conveniently approach the larger question of the Christian use of the Old Testament by first applying some of our general guidelines to the Old Testament in particular, for example the necessary attention to language and translation. Readers who 'have sat at a feast of languages and have gathered up the scraps', and who in consequence can say 'he said' in more ways than are possible in any other tongue, can scarcely understand the limitations of Hebrew, which has hardly a dozen rules of grammar, and so few words available that any one might carry up to twenty meanings. Translation can be quite adventurous! A language so simple, vivid, pictorial, childlike, must never be pressed to yield precise statement, strict logic, or subtlety of thought.

Add the difficulties of writing Hebrew on perishable papyrus, and the laborious process of copying, and the innumerable footnotes, 'Hebrew obscure', 'correction' (or 'Cn'), and the countless occasions when the oldest of all translations (the Greek 'Septuagint', the LXX) differs from the Hebrew, are explained. It is obviously nonsense to argue fine theological points from the niceties of Old Testament expressions. The Old Testament way of putting things, even where it is clear, is neither philosophical, legal nor theological, but poetic, allusive, descriptive, sometimes childish. That is part of its great charm.

Any competent modern printing of the Bible warns readers by its layout how much of the scripture is in actual poetry. Long passages of the prophets, as well as *Psalms, Job, Song of Solomon*, and much else, are poems whose structure, division into stanzas, and emotional tone (lyrical, joyous, rousing, mourning, penitent) all affect interpretation. It helps, sometimes, to realise we are reading poetry and not sober prose; occasionally, we should pay special attention when short (and perhaps later) comments interrupt a poem, using prose. Sometimes a passage becomes clearer if we recall that poets do not always draw attention to a change of speaker. With this in mind, it becomes obvious that throughout the *Song of*

Solomon a conversation is going on. In Psalm 91, it looks as though some over-confidence of the poet ('He will deliver you . . . it will not come near you . . . no evil shall befall you . . .') is answered (note the change of speaker in verse 14) by God: 'I will be with him *in* trouble, I will rescue him'. In Isaiah 53, too, the testimony of the prophet to the Servant of the Lord is answered by God himself in verse 12 — 'Therefore I will divide him a portion with the great . . .'

The chief characteristic of Hebrew poetry is not rhymed sounds at the end of lines, but rhymed thoughts —

> Blessed is the man that walketh not in the
>   counsel of the ungodly
> Nor standeth in the way of sinners
> Nor sitteth in the seat of the scornful . . .
> Every valley shall be lifted up,
>   And every mountain and hill be made low;
> The uneven ground shall become level,
>   And the rough places a plain . . .

Sometimes the second or third way of saying the same thing is very cleverly varied — to provide contrast, to offer illustration, to carry the thought a shade further, then further, or even to suggest a balancing thought: always this 'parallelism' lends emphasis and richness to poetic expression. Very frequently, too, it assists interpretation, when an obscure word occurs, or even when a word or line has dropped out, and the parallel pattern supplies the clue to what is meant.

Another poetic device is the acrostic, where lines or groups of lines follow the Hebrew alphabet, as in *Lamentations*, Psalm 119. We would not expect here to find deep connections between successive thoughts, but rather variations upon a theme, each suggested by the wholly artificial pattern of the poem.

Variety of religious approach must be allowed for

in the Old Testament as fully as in the New. God is revealed not only in the more obvious ways of history, law, prophecy and worship, but in the tensions between the advancing civic culture, influenced by foreign example, and the older, nomadic 'puritan' tradition of the pious guilds (Rechabites, Nazarites and others); and again in the so-called Wisdom School which aimed to bring the essential practical wisdom of 'the fear of the Lord' to the attention of those repelled by law, ritual and 'priestcraft', in literature like *Proverbs*, *Job*, *Ecclesiastes* and some psalms. To interpret correctly, such variety of statement must be acknowledged, though the same central truths are reached from each approach.

But of all the general guidelines, perhaps it is the need of true historical perspective which most affects interpretation of the Old Testament, and which is oftenest misunderstood. It is hard for some Christians to believe that Israel knew God, or that God dealt with Israel in truth and mercy long before Christ came. The so-called 'Christological' interpretation of the Old Testament too often assumes that all that God did or said in Israel's experience had validity or value only long afterwards in pointing forward to Christ. In this way some Christians, while professing to 'believe the Bible from cover to cover', rob two-thirds of it of all contemporary relevance and truth.

Yet the author of Psalm 139 certainly knew God's companionship; Samuel and Jeremiah certainly spoke God's truth to their own generation; those who brought sacrifices to the altar as God directed certainly experienced divine mercy. When a lawyer asked Jesus the secret of inheriting eternal life, Jesus invited him to quote the commandments, adding 'Do this, and you will live' — just as Paul was later to declare that the commandments promised life (Luke 10:25–28; **Rom. 7:10**). There are those who prefer to

calculate the probable number of pips in the
pomegranates that decorated the High Priest's robes
and arrive at the 144,000 of Revelation 7:4, than to
believe that anyone for whom the High Priest prayed
received any divine blessing! But it is not by denying
the genuineness of others' experience of God that the
interpreter of the Old Testament divines the truth:
but by acknowledging that that experience was *both*
true and genuine in itself *and* a stage on the way to
fuller knowledge of God in Christ.

For (as we have already stressed) the Old
Testament shows both the direct relevance of each
divine revelation to its own generation and its need,
and the growth in moral and spiritual understanding
which the passing generations enjoyed. The earlier
corporate responsibility is later balanced by
emphasis on individual guilt; arguments against the
worship of the fertility gods of Canaan give place to
Isaiah's marvellous ironic tirade against the
developed idolatry of paganism; the local seer with
'second sight', able to help in finding lost property
gives place to the political commentator speaking in
God's name (1 Sam. 9:6-10); and the repeated failure
of all other expedients made ever clearer the
necessity for direct divine intervention in a coming
saviour, if mankind was ever to be redeemed.

Variety of approach, and changing historical
circumstances, between them account for most of the
apparent inconsistencies in the teaching of the Old
Testament: the pessimism of *Ecclesiastes* contrasted
with the joy of Psalm 16, for example; the counsel of
Jeremiah that the exiles should settle down and make
the best of Babylon, contrasted with the efforts of
Isaiah to rouse them to return home (Jer. 29:4-9; Isa.
40) — and so much more.

The historical background, the dates of books, and
the *movement forward* in God's revelation of his
purposes must therefore always be considered when
we seek the meaning of any passage in the Old

Testament. But not everything comes as clear as we might wish. *Deuteronomy*, which tradition holds to be by Moses, requires the centralisation of worship in one place, and breathes the broad humanitarian spirit engendered by the social conscience of the later prophets. If the book was indeed by Moses, then Eli, Samuel, and Elijah defied God's law in sacrificing at various places; and the contrast between the earlier legislation and this 'second version of the law' is inexplicable. The book found in the temple in Josiah's time led to precisely such changes as *Deuteronomy* prescribes: it is a persuasive theory that that book was our *Deuteronomy*.

Again, doubtless God *could* have revealed to Isaiah in Jerusalem in the eighth century BC the name of the next world-conqueror but one who at the end of the exile, about two centuries later, would restore Judah to her homeland; and with the name (Cyrus), also the numerous stirring calls to leave Babylon and return home. But the revelation could have neither meaning nor purpose for Isaiah's hearers; Isaiah in fact assured Judah that Jerusalem would not be destroyed; and Jeremiah, following Isaiah, seems to have known nothing of any promised deliverer. If however the chapters in *Isaiah* heralding the return from exile belong to the years just before that return, all their exhortations, promises and warnings came to those who needed them, and a distinct change of style and vocabulary tends to confirm this. We remain puzzled that the messages of different men in different times should have come down to us as one book of '*Isaiah*': but as with all such questions, *the light which revised dating throws upon the meaning and relevance of the contents* is the best argument for keeping an open mind.

Of the larger questions affecting Christian handling of the Old Testament, the central one is: Granting that Jesus knew, loved and used thoroughly the sacred literature of his people, what was his own attitude towards it? The answer is somewhat surprising.

Most familiar is Jesus' deliberate setting over against 'what you have heard was said by them of old time' his own 'but I say unto you'. It is not only traditional interpretations of the Old Testament which he here sets aside, but the inadequacy of its actual requirements: 'Thou shalt not commit adultery', 'Thou shalt not kill' fail to prohibit (as Jesus points out) the states of mind that make such actions possible. The new Christian ideal here excels and supersedes the Old Testament standard.

Familiar too is his selective emphasis, as he demands that ritual matters — like the washing of hands up to the elbow, the meticulous avoidance even of humanitarian labour on the sabbath — shall give place to the moral requirements of each situation, the cleansing of the heart, compassion towards the hungry and the sick. The implications of this attitude must not be minimised: quite deliberately Jesus underlines some Old Testament requirements and sets aside others: 'If you had known what this means, "I desire mercy and not sacrifice", you would not have condemned the guiltless.' What then of *Leviticus*? Here the new Christian truth fulfils and removes part of Old Testament teaching.

But Christ's sovereign discrimination in the use of the Old Testament goes much further than this. A sermon which began with gracious exposition of a passage from Isaiah ended in uproar when Jesus drew from the stories of Elijah and Naaman lessons on God's care for Gentiles which were not to that congregation's taste. Equally provocative was the use he made of Isaiah's great parable of the vineyard: Jews were used to the rebuke that after all the care God had lavished on his chosen people, they had failed to bear fruit; they had never heard, and from their outspoken objections they were not

prepared to hear, that God would take the vineyard
from them and give it to others (Luke 20:9–16). That
was not in Isaiah, but Jesus found the implication
there, and repeated it in the Upper Room when he
declared that he and his men, not Israel, were the
vine of God.

Still more radical was Jesus' readiness to expose
inner contrasts of attitude within the Old Testament.
Against the strict law governing the sabbath he set
the provision for the circumcision of infants on the
sabbath day — a conflict of principles which
required considerable casuistry to explain away.
Against the insistence that the divine rules must be
observed at all times he set the example of David
distributing the sacred shewbread (reserved by
regulation for the priests) among his soldiers, hunger
taking   precedence   over   ritual.   And   very
significantly,   when   challenged   about   Moses'
provision of divorce for dissatisfied husbands, Jesus
calmly set over against the Mosaic concession to the
hardness of men's hearts (as he called it) the original
divine intention as expressed in *Genesis*, that a man
shall so cleave to his wife as to become one flesh with
her.

Radical   discrimination   between   passage   and
passage is revealed too in Christ's answer to the
current question about which of all the hundreds of
requirements in the sacred law was the most
important. To say 'Love God and your neighbour'
was in itself a courageous evaluation of priorities; to
add, as Jesus did, 'On these hang all the law and the
prophets' was to invite a charge of blasphemy
against all the Old Testament except two verses!

Once at least, in a suggestion about calling down
fire upon inhospitable Samaritans 'as Elijah did', and
probably twice, despite the doubt where the story of
the woman taken in adultery originally belonged,
scripture was quoted to Jesus to guide his own
actions. In each case he ignored what the scripture

said, framing his own response on quite different principles.

In one other central matter, so familiar that we tend to miss its enormous importance, Jesus rejected one Old Testament expectation in favour of another, wholly contrary in meaning. The Davidic ideal was the prevailing category in which the hope of Messiah was framed by nearly all interpreters of the Old Testament in Christ's day, even though they differed on how he would appear. John the Baptist pictured Messiah as coming in power and judgement, with axe, flail, and flaming torch, for which Old Testament precedents might be found. Yet Jesus challenged the whole concept.

'How can the scribes say that the Christ is the son of David?' he demanded on one occasion (Mark 12:35) — and we cannot seriously suppose he was merely setting a conundrum in the art of exegesis. 'What do you think of the Christ, whose son is he?' is Matthew's version of the question, implying that their expectation of a Messiah in David's likeness could be wholly wrong. To place the challenge to inherited Old Testament ideas beyond doubt, he himself chose instead the image of the suffering Servant, ministering to God and men by giving his life a ransom for many, as the true picture of the person and work of the Messiah.

In the light of all this, it is false to say that Jesus accepted every word of the Old Testament as in equal degree the inspired and authoritative word of God for his own soul. His deep love and reverence for the scriptures did not at all silence the voice of God within himself, or the moral discrimination he exercised over what he read. The question remains, whether a similar freedom of interpretation and selective emphasis is afforded by his example to those who follow him.

To assert that it is would be to make every man his own Christ, and destroy the authority of the Old

c

Testament altogether. But that some discrimination, in the light of Jesus' attitude, is necessary can hardly be doubted: and the mere feeling that this or that is permanently binding upon conscience, and other things are not, is hardly sufficient. We need directives that safeguard reverence while allowing responsible freedom.

(i) It seems trite to say that everything in the Old Testament is pre-Christian. If Christ be indeed the final and perfect revelation of God's mind and will, then everything in the Old Testament is sub-Christian, too. Obviously, that does not imply that everything is unchristian: countless passages, prayers, moral examples, biographies, principles, glimpses of God's ways, testimonies to God's goodness, have a permanent value. Christianity itself has not produced a finer expression of confidence in God than Psalm 23, or a profounder confession of sin than Psalm 51; a more wonderful assertion of divine companionship than Psalm 139, nor a more inspiring analysis of the springs of religious comfort than Isaiah 40. There is no question that the Old Testament provides still for every Christian a remarkable education in the understanding of God, a discipline of the deepest devotion, a moral syllabus of precedent, counsel, warning and biography.

Yet some things give one pause: the poison-cup test for adultery, the burning of witches, wholesale destruction of men, women and children, homes and villages in the occupation of Canaan (so airily 'explained' by mild and cultured evangelical professors, glancing over their pince-nez, as 'because the Canaanites were dreadful sinners', without the slightest suspicion that Jesus, in that case, had got God all wrong!). Other details of the Old Testament Christians themselves have misused. Some of Jerome's counsel to virgins borders on the pornographic, based on the sexual imagery of the *Song of Solomon*; some arguments about slavery, war, the 'churching of women after childbirth', the exclusion of women from Christian ministry, apartheid, are only made palatable at all to Christian minds by being represented as 'scriptural', on the assumption that all the Old Testament is equally binding as Christian scripture.

If it be remembered that such stumbling towards moral insight is pre-Christian, subject therefore to re-appraisal in the light of Christ, it occasions no difficulty: exalted as divine law for modern Christian life, such ideas become abhorrent. Refusal to exercise Christian moral discrimination in such matters amounts to saying that the world after all did not need Jesus to show the will of God more clearly. All we urge is that the Old Testament is for Christianity *preparatory* and temporary, rather than essential and permanent. The New Testament on the other hand is final, in some sense still to be discussed: it is not to be followed by a third 'Testament', nor made 'obsolete' (compare Heb. 8:13) by further revelation. To see the Old Testament as introduction to, and illuminating commentary upon, the New Testament is very different from binding upon the Christian conscience all that the Old Testament says.

(ii) Christian discrimination in the use of the Old Testament must therefore take account of the fact that a considerable part of the New Testament is devoted to breaking the link between Christianity and the older faith: *Matthew, John*, parts of *Acts, Romans, Galatians* and Philippians 3 all argue the differences, and the liberation of Christian believers from Judaism. It was one of the main tasks of the apostle Paul to disentangle the permanent heritage of truth, morality and hope which Christianity conserved, from the ritualistic, legalistic and nationalist features of Judaism from which Christ delivered us.

Jesus declared that the righteousness of the

disciples must exceed that of the scribes and
Pharisees (Matt. 5:20): the moral principles of the
Jewish law, as newly interpreted by Christ, remain
binding on the Christian conscience. Paul argues that
the righteousness which the Jewish law could not
achieve must be attained by the Christian in another
way, by the rule of the Spirit of life in Christ Jesus
(Rom. 8:2-4). Christ is the end of the law so far as the
attainment of righteousness before God is concerned,
for all who believe in Jesus (Rom. 10:4): the Christian
lives by faith which is counted to him for
righteousness (Rom. 4:22-24), and in place of the
Jewish law the basis of all relationship with God is
now faith in Christ, crucified and risen, and life in
the Spirit. Hence the ancient Jewish food tabus,
national customs, ritual regulations, circumcision,
sabbath and the rest were not to be imposed upon
new converts, called to the liberty of the Spirit in
Christ.

A parallel argument in *Hebrews* contends that the
Christian possesses a more authoritative revelation
(through a son, not a servant), a superior High Priest
and mediator, a more perfect rest, an altar, a
sacrifice, a covenant, an access to God and an
example of faith, greater than anything which
Judaism could offer. All that mattered in Judaism
was conserved in Christianity, being fulfilled in
Christ.

Moreover, the rejection and crucifixion of Christ
by leaders and adherents of the older faith was no
mere accident or mistake. A breach with Judaism
was inevitable: this must be remembered when any
attempt is made to impose Jewish principles upon
Christian hearts.

(iii) One important aspect of this disentanglement
of Christianity from Judaism is frequently overlooked
by those whose great interest in Old Testament
prophecy leads them to unfold detailed programmes
of the future in which the racial, religious and

national unit of 'Israel' figures very largely. The chief weakness of many such schemes is that they make Christ and his work entirely irrelevant, even superfluous: the Jew is represented as having some guaranteed place in God's purposes on the basis of race, irrespective of his attitude to Christ. Many such schemes also depend upon lifting words of the prophets wholly out of their literary and historical context, ignoring their original meaning. And they also ignore the crucial redefinition of who are 'Israel', which the New Testament works out.

John the Baptist explicitly refuted the claim that to be sons of Abraham was sufficient to ensure a place in the messianic kingdom. Jesus quite clearly and repeatedly envisaged the inclusion of Gentiles in the people of God to whom the divine vineyard will be entrusted (Matt. 8:10,11; 24:14; 28:19; Luke 20:16; compare John 10:16; 11:51,52). And Paul roundly declared that 'He is not a real Jew who is one outwardly . . . He is a Jew who is one inwardly' (Rom. 2:28,29). Paul is prepared to claim that Abraham is the father of all, in all nations, who have faith (Rom. 4:16,17), and even to argue that God shows no partiality between Jew and Gentile, apparently thereby cancelling out any thought of national election; for though the Jew had had advantages, he did not benefit from them (Rom. 2:9–11; 3:1,2,9).

In short, Paul contends that it is for God to decide who are 'Israel': 'It is not as though the word of God had failed. For not all who are descended from Israel belong to Israel, and not all are children of Abraham because they are his descendants . . . What shall we say then? Is there injustice on God's part? By no means! For he says to Moses, I will have mercy on whom I have mercy, and I will have compassion on whom I have compassion . . . So then he has mercy upon whomever he wills, and he hardens the heart of whomever he wills' (Rom. 9:6–18 abbreviated).

It is true that in order to curb overweening pride

on the part of the Gentiles in a mixed church, Paul
would have them remember Israel's special place in
the outworking of salvation, and their own debt to
'Israel after the flesh' (Rom. 11:17–25). But when he
writes to Gentile Philippians he says positively, 'We
are the true circumcision' (3:3); and in the end he
lays it down that 'There is neither Jew nor Greek . . .
you are all one in Christ Jesus. And if you are
Christ's, then you are Abraham's offspring, heirs
according to promise' (Gal. 3:28,29; and so, again,
Rom. 10:12,13).

It makes a great muddle of many zealous prophetic
programmes to apply this revised New Testament
definition to 'the chosen people'. God's promises will
be fulfilled — but he will say to whom. He will have
mercy on whom he has mercy: all, now and in the
future, is of grace, and all is through Christ.

Christianity's break with Judaism was not of
course complete; a deep indebtedness remains.
Perhaps some things were inherited that might have
been better left behind: a priestly conception of
ministry rests on Old Testament rather than New
Testament ground; a militarist conception of
Messiah, who will in wrath destroy the wicked, owes
more to David than to Jesus; Jewish ideas of salvation
through natural descent (echoed in infant baptism),
of State religion, and some remnants of Jewish
attitudes towards women, and race, linger in
Christianity.

But far greater riches came from Old Testament
teaching — the fundamental concept of God as one,
holy, sovereign, creator, and judge; the indissoluble
unity of religion with morality, Israel's main
contribution to the religion of the world; an emphasis
upon corporate religious experience. The creation
doctrine kept religion in close and healthy touch with
man's natural life; and the idea of God as Lord of
history lent a purpose and a goal to man's existence.
The later Old Testament idea of God as living Spirit
likewise bore rich fruit in Christianity.

Within these general truths, the very foundations of the Christian faith, lie three others which have determined Christian thought from the beginning. Israel's chequered experience of human kings, which nourished her hope of a divinely anointed king or Messiah, set one pattern for understanding Jesus. Israel's system of worship, assuming the holiness of God and the necessity of sacrificial atonement, yet ever dissatisfied with animal sacrifice (Ps. 51; Isa. 1:12-20; Micah 6:6-8) set another category within which Jesus' work might be interpreted. And the notion of the supreme sacrifice of the suffering Servant of God and man gave to Jesus himself the model for his mission for mankind.

It is not in a jigsaw puzzle of hints, types and prophetic prefigurings that the 'fulfilment' of the Old Testament lies, but in the deepest religious assumptions of the New Testament faith, experience, morality and worship, and above all in these central ideas of Messiah, sacrifice and Servant of the Lord. For that reason, as well as for educational and devotional purposes, the Old Testament retains its abiding value for the Christian reader.

A supplementary guideline for the Old Testament should pursue this idea of 'fulfilment' into the centuries between the Testaments. It is sometimes assumed, quite falsely, that one passes out of the Old Testament into the New to find all clear, intelligible, and prepared. In fact we find the Romans in occupation of Palestine; people called scribes, Pharisees, Sadducees, Herodians, zealots have appeared on the scene; Hellenists (Greek educated Jews) betray a Greek period in Israel's history; while beyond the borders of Palestine exists a widely 'Dispersed' Jewry settled in pagan lands. New ideas are under discussion too: resurrection and immortality, Hades, a zeal for making proselytes among the pagans, together with a new exclusiveness that emphasised everything Jewish and nationalist. The later books of the Wisdom

School, and the struggles of the Maccabean age, have left marks discernible in the picture of Jewry in the New Testament; while a new school of apocalyptists look for a 'son of man' to appear on the clouds. A non-conforming Judaism, radical and monastic in type, has appeared in the Essenes and the settlements around the Dead Sea, and for these, as the ministry and message of the Baptist suggests, Jesus might have had a special attractiveness.

For none of these changes does the Old Testament prepare us. It is not suggested that every Bible reader must become competent in the tangled history of the inter-testamental period: but it is well to remember the considerable lapse of time between the Testaments, and the fertile and turbulent developments within that time. God was not unknown, or idle, in those years, and the serious student should feel some curiosity concerning the later preparation for Christ. In the same way, conscientious teachers should be fairly heard when they appeal to events and changes that appear to be 'outside' the Bible, but which were in reality 'between the Testaments'. (For a brief conspectus of the more tangled parts of Old Testament history, showing which prophets served in the time of which kings, see page 122 foll.)

5

Guidelines for the Gospels

The Gospels bring us to the very heart of scripture, to the feet of him who is the living word of God, the Lord of scripture. The Gospels make their own impact on the reverent reader; here most of all the heart listens, with little need to be told what to listen for. Yet some background information, and some care in handling the most sacred pages of the Bible, serve only to illumine their meaning and to release their power.

We begin, again, with the particular application of our general guidelines. In the sayings of Jesus, the difficulties attending translation are doubled by a preliminary translation out of the Aramaic (the common spoken 'Hebrew' of Palestine) in which Jesus taught, first into the Greek of our Gospels, and then out of Greek into English, with some loss of precision, some danger of inaccuracy, at each step. A few of the Master's actual Aramaic expressions, indeed, have survived the double translation and come into English unchanged: 'Ephatha', 'Abba', 'Talitha cumi'.

There existed no 'authorised' Greek version of the utterances of Jesus. Each translated as best he could, which may account for some of the variations in the record of his sayings. Matthew's 'If a blind man leads a blind man, both will fall into a pit' becomes in Luke's version 'Can a blind man lead a blind man? Will they not both fall into a pit?' — a difference sufficiently explained by variant translation (Matt. 15:14; Luke 6:39). The same fact may explain a few puzzles.

A centurion assures Jesus that he too is a man under authority, giving as proof his ability to say to one 'Go' and he goes — which sounds odd: the Aramaic word for 'under' can mean 'in place of', too (Matt. 8:9). 'Do not give dogs what is holy; and do not throw your pearls before swine' (Matt. 7:6) supposes a very strange proceeding: a very similar Aramaic word, plus help from Hebrew parallelism, has suggested that Jesus said, 'Give not a costly ring to dogs, nor cast your pearls before swine'. On outward and inward cleanness, Jesus says in Luke 11:41 'Give for alms those things which are within; and behold, everything is clean for you' — which again sounds very odd. A single-letter change in an Aramaic word would yield 'Cleanse what is within (the heart) then all is pure', which is not only clearer, but agrees with Matthew 23:26. On the other hand, in each case the Aramaic original has to be conjectured, and 'unfamiliarity of Aramaic to Greek translators' must not be used to explain every difficulty.

More positively, Aramaic words sometimes possess nuances that are lost in translation into Greek. The most important example, probably, is the word 'kingdom', which in Aramaic cannot represent the area, or organisation, of a physical kingdom, the land, people, cities, economy, but only the king's active ruling, his imposing laws and directing affairs. That is why Moffat always translated the phrase so often on Christ's lips as 'the reign of God': 'the kingdom' certainly seeks the will of God in all the affairs of the world and every side of the Christian's life, but its essence lies in the surrender of trustful hearts to the 'reign of God' within.

In the sayings of Jesus, again, it is especially important to 'read what is there'. Many ideas attributed to the Master are in fact misquotations or distortions of his words. He never defended the thoughtless improvidence which never thinks ahead: he did say 'Be not anxious (full of care) about tomorrow'. He never advised society to turn the other cheek or forego justice where crime is committed: he did call upon individuals to accept suffering rather than to inflict it, and never to seek revenge. Jesus never suggested one should be 'unwordly' about others' poverty, or counsel contentment to the starving: he did urge that each should be content with his own lot — and God; that ambition could disappoint, riches disappear through theft, moth and rust, and that to spend one's soul to gain the world was a fool's bargain.

Moreover, Jesus was certainly no naive idealist, moving starry-eyed in a world of angels sadly misunderstood, irradiated by charitable make-believe: a study of his parables reveals a whole gallery of rogues, dishonest, lazy, envious, loveless, proud, self-righteous, exploiters of others, vengeful, self-excusing, embezzling, ungrateful fools, worldlings — there is more ground for charging him with cynicism about men, than with sentimentalism.

Nor did Jesus ever set aside the strict moral requirements of the divine will. 'Unless your righteousness exceeds that of the scribes and Pharisees, you will never enter the kingdom of heaven' is a dreadful warning; 'till heaven and earth pass away, not an iota, not a dot, will pass from the law until all is accomplished.' And so far from lowering that towering standard of morality, Jesus actually raised it, and pressed it inward upon the secret places of the soul.

Nor, once again, did Jesus ever suggest that the way of the disciple would be sheltered from trouble or free of adversity; or that faith and godliness guaranteed happiness, an emotional 'jag' of perpetual excitements and everlasting joy. He called men to sit down first and count the cost of following him; he repulsed thoughtless offers of discipleship; and he warned explicitly that *the same* rain, and wind, and flood would beat upon the house of the man who heard and obeyed his words, as beat on the house of the man who heard and ignored: the difference lay in what would survive life's storm.

Examples abound of things Jesus is 'supposed' to have said, but never did or would have said. In no area of scripture is the simple counsel to attend to what is written more rewarding, or more challenging.

Nevertheless it is necessary to recall also the general guideline urging respect for highly imaginative language. It is possible that Jesus himself often saw truth in pictorial form, as expressed in his comment upon the jubilant return of the disciples from their mission, 'I saw Satan fall like lightning from heaven', and in his own description of the wilderness temptation. He certainly enshrined truth in metaphors, images, tales, pictures and similes, which often cannot be taken literally, *but must always be taken seriously.*

We can hardly suppose that Jesus advised the tempted actually to dismember hands and feet and to pluck out their eyes to avoid sin — though Origen took it quite literally, and mutilated himself to 'cure' lust. Yet such an idea runs counter to Christ's whole healing ministry, as well as to his view of sin as of the heart. Nor can we take literally his advice to sell our shirts and buy swords, when Jesus warned only minutes later that he who takes the sword will perish by the sword, and later again told Pilate that his kingdom is not of this world 'else would my servants fight'.

It is highly improbable that Jesus promised that the disciples should sit — literally — on twelve thrones judging the twelve tribes of Israel, if only because the

terms of such a promise include Judas. But it would
also contradict all Jesus said, both in public and to
James and John, about the real nature of the kingdom
and its cost in suffering and denial. Improbable, too
(though here we may feel less assurance), is the
advice to seek a fish with a coin in its mouth in order
to meet tax demands. We are not told a miracle
happened, and if it had done, it would be the only
miracle Jesus ever worked for himself. It seems
likelier that the figurative words mean — 'You ask
me for money, when you are a fisherman, and there
is the sea!' Only a literalist, western mind would
want it so spelled out.

Here again, accustomed Bible readers have little
difficulty in subtracting the metaphor from the
meaning. But let any one propose to do the same with
Jesus' vivid picture of a soul punished by its own
corruption, the picture based upon the valley of
Hinnom where Jerusalem's rubbish was tipped,
including offal from the temple sacrifices, and where
in consequence fire smouldered continually and
maggots bred unendingly, and protests will arise that
'modernism is denying Jesus' teaching on the eternal
destruction of the wicked! Yet 'Gehenna, where their
worm does not die and the fire is not quenched' is a
perfect figure (borrowed from Isaiah 66:24) for the
final corruption and permanent loss in store for the
unredeemed. To insist upon understanding it literally
raises the problem that what is eternal cannot be
also destroyed, nor what is destroyed remain
eternal!

If we are not careful to observe the dramatic,
imaginative style of Jesus' sayings, we shall make
him responsible for hatred of their parents by young
Christian converts; for avoidance of all shared
prayer — since he said 'go into your room and shut
the door and pray to your father who is in secret'; for
the drowning of men, with millstones fastened about
their necks; and for repeated shifting of mountains

about the scenery by prodigious acts of geographical faith.

It is possible to argue that Jesus had also the poet's facility with words as well as the artist's eye for pictures; for here and there his teaching falls very easily into the Hebrew poetic form, complete with paralleled thoughts. For this reason, some of his sayings are well-nigh unforgettable, once really heard. Who that has *listened* to 'Ask and it shall be given you; seek, and you will find; knock, and it will be opened unto you; for every one that asks receives, and he that seeks finds, and to him who knocks it will be opened' will ever forget it again? It may be that this 'poetic' aspect of his sayings was so common a teaching device amidst a non-reading people that we should think rather of mnemonics than of poetry: but the rhythm is very clear in many of his words, whichever explanation we prefer.

Turning now to the foundation for any special guidelines to the interpretation of the Gospels, we must ask the nature of these uniquely precious books. The first thing to be said is that the Gospels were written to distil, and so to replace, the testimony of eyewitnesses of Christ's ministry. The chief motive for writing lay in the passing of the first generation. Mark and Luke were associates of apostles; it is possible that in their final form the Gospels of Matthew and John, too, bear the handprints of associates of apostles: but it is almost certain that the contents in each case represent the testimony, immediate or reflective, of Matthew, Peter, Paul and John.

Luke tells us that many such attempts were made to record Christian origins, most of them unsatisfactory; for he suggests they were not sufficiently researched, nor written in orderly fashion (Luke 1:1-4). John tells us that all such accounts are necessarily incomplete, for there are many things Jesus said and did which are not recorded, and he adds 'were every one of them to be written, I suppose that the world itself could not contain the books that would be written' (John 20:30; 21:25). It is hardly surprising therefore that some sayings of Jesus have been preserved outside the Gospels: 'those who proclaim the gospel should get their living by the gospel' (1 Cor. 9:14); 'It is more blessed to give than to receive' (Acts 20:35).

It would be of the greatest interest if we could discover that some 'sayings of Jesus' from outside the New Testament altogether were genuine: to a man working on the sabbath, 'Man, if indeed thou knowest what thou art doing, thou art blessed: but if thou knowest not, thou art accursed'; 'Never rejoice except when you have looked on your brother in love'; 'He who is near me is near the fire: he who is far from me is far from the kingdom'. Again, 'Wherever there are two, they are not without God: and wherever there is one alone, I say I am with him. Raise the stone, and there thou shalt find me; cleave the wood and there am I'; 'Life is a bridge, seek not to build upon it'.

The third fact to bear in mind is that the basic source of the Gospels lies in innumerable personal memories about Jesus, treasured in individual hearts, families, villages, groups, told and retold hundreds of times, arranged and re-arranged in memory, and (as the records clearly show) inevitably varying somewhat in the telling. This is hardly surprising, since it was some thirty years before the earliest of our Gospels was penned (Mark), plenty of time for memories to fade, become confused, and the telling to affect the tale. Nor is it surprising that the best preserved of these reminiscences of Jesus should be those in the forms most easily recalled, dramatic miracles, moving parables, and arguments in which Jesus was plainly the victor.

Naturally, the stories most often repeated were those which helped the early Christians to

understand Christ's mind and will, about paying
taxes to a pagan State, about marriage, the sabbath,
prayer, about the right attitude towards outsiders,
Gentiles, enemies; and about the future. In this way
the memories were sifted by the daily needs of the
Christian community in its immediate situation
within Jewry, and later within paganism. 'What did
the Master say . . .?': if we do not possess all that
Jesus said and did, we have that which the first
Christians found urgently relevant to their lives and
problems.

Many of the Jesus-stories, therefore, focus upon
some clear pronouncement which Christians needed
to remember: 'The sabbath was made for man, not
man for the sabbath'; 'Render to Caesar the things
that are Caesar's, and to God the things that are
God's'; 'What therefore God has joined together, let
no man put asunder'. Sometimes with these
pronouncements there is preserved sufficient of the
occasion and context to show how they came to be
made; sometimes only the sayings themselves
survive, detached from any immediate circumstances, resulting in the brief epigrams we know so
well: 'Unto him who has shall more be given . . .'; 'If
the salt has lost its savour, wherewith shall it be
salted?'

In the process of teaching, Christ's deeds and
words naturally became grouped for memorising; in
the process of compiling the separate memories into
connected accounts, too, sayings and incidents not
originally belonging together in time or place became
linked and grouped for convenience. It is dangerous
to speculate overmuch in this way, but here and
there the artificial connection seems too obvious to
miss, and recognition of it assists our interpretation.

If we compare, for example, the sayings of Jesus in
Matthew's long 'sermon on the mount' with Luke's
account of those same sayings, it becomes very clear
that Matthew has grouped together utterances
which Luke shows were spoken on different

occasions. Luke says the pattern of the Lord's prayer was given upon request of the disciples for instruction after listening to Jesus praying 'in a certain place'; Matthew places the pattern-prayer in a whole section of the sermon on the mount which deals with almsgiving, prayer and fasting in secret, and spoken to 'the crowds' on the hillside. Again, Luke gives the sayings about laying up treasure in heaven, where nothing destroys, because where your treasure is there will be your heart, as a comment added to the parable of the rich fool, itself spoken in response to a request to arbitrate between brothers over property. Matthew gives all these sayings as part of the mountain sermon.

This compilation of originally separate sayings almost certainly explains at least three familiar perplexities. At the end of Mark 9 there is a series of sayings which no reverent ingenuity can weave into a coherent discourse. Warning against making 'little ones' *offend* leads to advice to sacrifice hand, foot or eye rather than *offend* and be cast into hell *fire*: because every one shall be salted (purified) with *fire* and *salt* is good, though if it lose its *saltness* it is irreparable. Have the *salt* of comradeship among yourselves, and be at peace. Clearly this is a collection of separate sayings linked by memory-words to aid recollection.

After the parable of the unjust steward Luke has recorded a number of sayings on the stewardship of wealth which just do not make sense if regarded as applications of the parable. The point which Jesus himself draws from the parable is simple: worldly people are so often more shrewd, intelligent and practical about making money than disciples are about the work of the kingdom (Luke 16:8). Stop there, and there is no difficulty. But try to draw further conclusions *from that story* — making friends, by means of money, with a view to eternal reward; he who is faithful in little, worldly things, is faithful in much (?spiritual things); to be unfaithful in worldly things is to be untrustworthy in spiritual things; none can serve two masters, God and mammon — and you confront a number of logical and ethical conundrums. The steward was not even handling his own money, nor was he hesitating between God and mammon, but between dismissal and blackmail. Nor was he comparing worldly and spiritual riches. Moreover, Matthew gives us the 'mammon' saying as part of the sermon on the mount! The whole connection of these isolated, unrelated sayings on stewardship with the parable they now follow is fortuitous, and unless we are alert readers, quite misleading.

An even clearer instance is Matthew's account of the great supper where, as the various sayings are now linked, some very odd things happen. The original guests making fatuous excuses, and even killing those who bring them invitations, servants are ordered to invite instead all they can find in the streets and lanes, 'good and bad'; yet when the royal host finds someone present in unsuitable garb, that guest is bound hand and foot and cast into outer darkness! Meantime, while the food is still on the table ('everything is ready') the king sent troops to assassinate the friends originally invited and destroy their city, before gathering in his new guests to food by this time cold and stale.

It is hard to find sense or justice in the present passage, and though dogmatism would be foolish, it does seem that two parables have become merged in the constant retelling before the written record was made. Once we recognise the method by which the Gospel writers compiled available oral reminiscences into connected accounts, it is possible to ask at numerous places whether the apparent connection — or incoherence — is due to the process of transmission, and not to anything Jesus originally said.

The selection and arrangement by which these 'Memoirs of the Apostles' as Justin Martyr called them were composed confronts us with two other features of Gospel writing which affect interpretation. One is the different use made of the same memories by different writers. That saying, for example, 'To every one who has will more be given, and he will have abundance; but from him who has not, even what he has will be taken away' (see Matt. 25:29) is attached in Matthew to the parable of the talents, and applied to the disciples' use in Christ's service of their varying capabilities. It means then that 'talents' used are increased thereby; those unused are diminished. In Matthew 13:12 the same words are attached to a saying about knowledge of the secrets of the kingdom, and they mean that knowledge attended to increases understanding, whereas knowledge neglected is lost. In Mark 4:25 the same words again are attached to the warning 'Take heed what you hear', and underline the responsibility of those to whom the gospel is preached: to hear with faith is to learn more; to hear carelessly is to become hardened. Has the aphorism been applied by the teaching church, or by the Gospel writers, in several directions, or did Jesus himself repeat it in different connections?

The saying, 'There is nothing hid, except to be made manifest, nor is anything secret, except to come to light' is connected by Mark (4:22; compare Luke 8:7) to the question whether a lamp is ever brought in to be placed under a wheat-bowl instead of on a candlestick: with Matthew 5:15 in mind, this idea seems related to Christian witness as 'lights shining in the world', and the temptation of the *disciple* to keep his faith dark. In Matthew 10:26 the same saying is connected with the coming experience of persecution, with the timidity which may keep the disciples silent when they should fearlessly proclaim upon the housetops what *Christ* has told in whispers and in the dark — because truth will out.

It is sometimes especially illuminating to observe

in this way the variant use of the same words of Jesus
by different Gospels. A good example is the way Luke
reproduces the 'beatitudes' in a literal and
uncomplicated form: 'Blessed are you poor, for yours
is the kingdom of God. Blessed are you that hunger
now, for you shall be satisfied; blessed are you that
weep . . . when men hate you . . .' This is followed by
woes upon those who have received their
consolation, upon the full, upon those who laugh,
those well spoken of. (James, too, treats the blessing
pronounced upon the poor as intended for those
literally poor, but rich in faith.) Matthew, as we all
know 'spiritualises' the blessed poor to mean 'poor in
spirit', and the hungry and thirsty as those yearning
'for righteousness' — a totally different meaning.

The parable of the lost sheep occurs in Luke as the
first of three by which Jesus defends his friendship
for tax-gatherers and sinners: it explains the motive
of the shepherd, who will go after even one lost sheep
until he finds it, as one sufficient motive for his
attitude towards lost souls. In Matthew, however,
the parable is placed in connection with the care of
'little ones who believe' (the 'weaker brethren of the
early church'?); with the dangers of temptation, the
restoration of the erring Christian brother within the
church fellowship, and the demand that we forgive *a
brother* without limit. The lost sheep is here, quite
clearly, the backsliding church member.

In 12:31, Matthew preserves a saying of Jesus
which many find quite bewildering. It follows an
accusation that Jesus is casting out demons by the
help of the prince of demons, and runs 'I tell you,
every sin and blasphemy will be forgiven men, but
blasphemy against the Spirit will not be forgiven.
And whoever says a word against the Son of man will
be forgiven; but whoever speaks against the Holy
Spirit will not be forgiven, either in this age or in the
age to come.' The warning is plainly serious, but
what can it mean? What is blasphemy against the

Holy Spirit, as distinct from blasphemy against the
Son of man, and why should it be beyond forgiveness,
if speaking against Christ is not?

Every attempted explanation seems incredibly
complicated. In Mark (3:28) we have a different
utterance in the same setting: 'All sins will be
forgiven the sons of men, and whatever blasphemies
they utter; but whoever blasphemes against the Holy
Spirit never has forgiveness, but is guilty of an
eternal sin.' And Mark explains that this was said
because 'they had said, "He has an unclean spirit".'
These final words leave no doubt that for Mark, the
blasphemy against the Spirit *is* blasphemy against
Christ; and the reason why there is no forgiveness is
precisely that, by confusing the Holy Spirit with
Satan and accusing Christ of being possessed by an
unclean spirit, the blasphemer reveals so deep a
moral blindness, so complete a confusion of right and
wrong, truth with falsehood, as to be beyond
repentance, and so beyond forgiveness. Whether
Matthew's inexplicable version of this arose from
someone's misreading, or misremembering, 'the sons
of men' as 'against the Son of man', can only be
conjectured.

These examples suffice to show that different
Gospel writers draw upon the common stock of
memories of Jesus in ways that vary both as to the
selection of what to record and as to the use made of
it. That *Matthew, Mark* and *Luke* are somehow inter-
related, beyond merely recounting the same general
story, now carries as much certainty as we might
hope for in such matters. All but thirty-one verses of
Mark is reproduced in *Matthew*-with-*Luke*, with
remarkable similarity in content, order and
language; while most of the remaining contents
which *Matthew* shares with *Luke* reveal so close
resemblance as to suggest a further common source
of some kind.

Without pursuing the two or three current theories

about this inter-relation, we may safely draw therefrom two further principles for sound Gospel-interpretation. One is, always compare the Gospels: never interpret an incident or saying in the Gospels without comparing one Gospel's account with any similar incident or saying in the other Gospels. God has given us *four* accounts of Jesus; if we conscientiously seek the meaning of anything Jesus said or did, we will diligently consult all four. A reference Bible will help us find related passages, but a 'parallel' edition of the four Gospels, which prints related or similar passages side by side, is an immense help.

The other principle of sound interpretation drawn from the inter-relation of the Gospels requires us to ask why *Matthew, Mark, Luke* and *John* use their source-material so differently. This involves, to be sure, some extensive study; but it is not difficult — provided we do not assume we know more than we do. It is obvious that each writes out of faith and with a view to faith — we have no 'neutral' or objective account of Jesus. Beyond that minimal concurrence in a Christian viewpoint, they diverge according to their situation and purpose.

Mark, a teacher in the Roman church, wrote (it is well-nigh certain) an account of Peter's preaching there, as Peter's life drew to a close. Deeds rather than words were remembered best; numerous Jewish customs and terms are explained for Gentile readers; there is little of interpretation — the portrait of the working Messiah, the Son of God, is allowed to speak for itself, though a stress on Christ's authority is clearly evident, appropriately for a church set at the seat of authority of a very different kind. Equally clear is the portrait of Christ in conflict, for a church already tasting Roman persecution. Much in *Mark* suggests the kind of instruction needed by converts in such a church as Rome, around 65 AD.

Matthew probably wrote some twenty years later, with a clear desire to supplement Mark's account of Christ's activity with much more on Christ's teaching. It is possible to show with considerable confidence that Matthew addressed himself to a church ethically confused and careless, needing therefore to hear again the searching moral message of Jesus; a church lacking spiritual power, and needing deeper faith in him who stands in glory within every church. By watching *how* Matthew tells the stories which Mark also tells, for example the healing of the woman with haemorrhage (where in *Matthew* the disciples and the crowd disappear altogether, and only Christ and the woman in conversation remain), or the stilling of the storm (where in *Matthew* the discussion of Christ's relation to his men, and Peter's venture of faith, precede the miracle), it is possible to discern where Matthew desires to lay his emphasis, and the message he finds within the stories for his own contemporaries.

One main purpose that emerges is to arm his readers, believers or not, for a sounder judgement on the claims of Jesus than was made by the generation of Jewish leaders who engineered his crucifixion: it is well-nigh certain that Matthew wrote, chiefly for Jews, about the time of the final breach of Christianity from Jewry by introduction of an anti-Christian benediction into the synagogue services. He evidently hoped still to persuade some Jews to recognise their Messiah, the greatest rabbi of them all, and to reassure any Christian Jews for whom the breach brought renewed searching of heart.

Luke uses the common material quite differently, having come upon Christianity first of all as expressed in the great mission church of the pagan world — a Spirit-filled, Spirit-empowered, Spirit-superintended pressure group with a pertinent and valuable social message for an empire facing considerable social and political problems. For Luke, himself a cultured Gentile, the chief task was to describe for cultured leaders of society (like 'his excellency' Theophilus Luke 1:3) this church of the Spirit, and present her case for legal recognition in the empire: this is plainly Luke's purpose in *Acts*. But in order to explain the origin of the whole Christian movement, Luke has to retell the story of Jesus as the coming of one born of the Spirit, bearing the Spirit, and bestowing the Spirit upon all who call upon him: this is clear from the way Jesus is introduced, the way the Gospel ends and the way that *Acts* begins.

John declares that he is writing a theological case (to show 'that Jesus is the Christ, the son of God') with a clearly evangelistic or confirming purpose — 'that you might believe' (or, 'go on believing') 'and have life in his name'. To that end John deliberately selects incidents in which Christ's self-revelation leads to faith, making the confession of Thomas the great climax of the story. With consummate skill, John addresses his account of Christ at every point to Jews, Greeks and other pagans by using language and conceptions that each group would understand — logos, wine-maker, shepherd, truth, eternal life, and the like. His resulting portrait of Christ differs much from that of *Matthew-Mark-Luke*, but fits perfectly into his declared purpose.

In other words, each of the Gospel writers is doing much more than preserving a record of what Jesus said and did in Palestine about 30–33 AD. Each is *also* addressing the church he knows, the church that is about him as he writes, with pastoral and evangelistic purpose. Each selects, arranges, emphasises, as suits himself, writing-up the story for his own readers, their time and their needs. Where Paul, facing current problems in the churches he knew, wrote *epistles*, Matthew, Mark, Luke and John wrote *Gospels*, deliberately taking their readers back to Jesus, to re-learn what they should have known from conversion, or to learn 'more accurately'

(as Luke says) what they had not got clear. And their
purpose too was pastoral: so that their readers might
understand Christ's mind more perfectly and follow
him more closely in the new circumstances of their
own discipleship.

This is no more, of course, than any modern
preacher and pastor is constantly doing as he
'applies Christ' to the problems of his own people.
But it does mean that in interpreting the Gospels we
must allow for their double time-reference: a
recalling of what Jesus said and did *then*, in the days
of his flesh, in order to affect how the church thinks
and lives *now*, as they read the Gospels in their own
time. The memories of Jesus are being applied in a
later age to new circumstances for a new audience:
that is often illuminating.

For an obvious example: when Jesus told the
parable of the Bridesmaids, in the streets of
Jerusalem (or wherever it was) towards the end of
his earthly ministry, it was plainly a warning to
recognise the Bridegroom already among them, to
put off slumber and be prepared for the messianic
feast offered to the nation. As yet, there was no
thought either in his hearers' minds or among the
disciples, of Messiah's rejection and death, let alone
of resurrection, and still less of a second coming to
earth. But when Matthew recalled the parable, half
a century later, for his contemporaries, the whole
situation had changed. The parable is then a
warning to be prepared for the delayed advent of
Christ. This is the theme of Matthew 24 to 25: 'the
end is not yet ... all this is but the beginning ...
Many false prophets will arise and lead many astray
... men's love will grow cold ... he who endures to
the end ... If any says, Lo, here is the Christ ... do
not believe it ... Of that day no one knows' (four
times) ... 'an hour you do not expect ... My master
is delayed ... the bridegroom was delayed ...'

Thus the point of the parable as Matthew uses it in

this context is not that Christ is coming soon, but that all must be prepared (as the sleeping girls were not) to cope with *delay*, to be ready *whenever* Christ comes. That was the word Matthew's colleagues needed. Passage after passage in the Gospels comes alive if we ask not only what does the writer tell us that Jesus said, but why does the writer tell it in that way, and what in the situation of the readers called for just that reminder? Once again, we are striving to read everything in its historical context — this time, in two contexts, that in which Jesus lived and spoke, and that in which the record was shaped and recorded.

Undoubtedly, the Gospels have marvellous power to make their point for the average alert and humble reader with no great background of knowledge or language: yet so precious are these four short books that no trouble should be too great to get their full force and meaning correct, and set free their message in congregations and in individual hearts.

6

Guidelines for the Epistles

What is an 'epistle'? Rather more than a letter, since
usually it is intended for wider than private reading,
and deals with more than personal matters. Epistles
were no Christian invention. The Greek rhetorical
schools used them to air in public the finer points of
their teaching; a speech of Demosthenes was so
'published', and the doctrines of Epicurus found
expression in epistles; others exist dealing with
geography, mathematics and politics. The epistle
was thus generally little more than a literary device
for discussion among widely separated scholars,
students and public figures: today, articles in
professional magazines fulfil a similar function. In
the New Testament, the epistle becomes an
instrument for communication between churches
and their leaders, though with various forms.

Polite correspondence in the first century followed
a pattern more sensible than ours. They *began* by
announcing who the letter was from, and naming
who it was for, followed by a word of greeting and
good wishes ('a good harvest to you, and a pleasant
holiday'); then an acknowledgement of the gods
(formal, or more earnest, and sometimes marking
specially holy days, or days of victory — 'The

gracious Venus be praised'; 'Thanks be to Mars the mighty!'). A prayer may follow ('I pray that you are better, and the baby coming on well'), and then at last the message, with more personal greetings at the end. The very brief letters mentioned in Acts 15:23 and 23:26 show some of these features but naturally not the full courtesies of more personal correspondence. The form may be seen quite closely followed, in Christian terms, in *Philippians* and *Colossians*, and with the prayer of thanksgiving and petition greatly elaborated, in *Ephesians*. Where the polite form is neglected, it is always worthwhile to ask why — for example *Galatians, Hebrews, 1 John.*

It is important, though, to notice how varied are the New Testament epistles. Some (*Philemon, 1 and 2 Timothy, Titus,* perhaps *2 and 3 John*) are to individuals; others (*1 and 2 Corinthians, 1 and 2 Thessalonians, Philippians, Colossians*) are addressed to particular churches for public reading. Yet others are sent to groups of churches: *1 Peter* (see 1:1); *Revelation* (see 1:4); *Galatians* ('the churches of Galatia' 1 Cor. 16:1), and (with some doubts) *Romans* (16:5 and 15 suggest different house-churches within the city congregation), are evidently meant to be circulated, or copied and distributed. Paul himself asks that his letter to Colossae be read also at Laodicea, in exchange for a letter sent there (Col. 4:16).

Ephesians, too, may be a circular. For Paul founded the church in Ephesus and spent three years there: yet he says he has 'heard' of their faith and love, and speaks of their having 'heard' of the stewardship of grace given to him (1:15; 3:2). If the letter were sent to Ephesus *and* its surrounding churches, this would be natural enough; the omission of the address ('at Ephesus' 1:2) from some important ancient manuscript copies may confirm this. A similar possibility arises concerning *Romans:* not only do some copies omit the address at 1:7 and 15, but copies vary greatly as to where the letter ends; besides, Paul seems to have known a lot of people in a church he had never visited, since he greets over thirty in chapter 16. Some have suggested that the substance of the Roman epistle was used for several churches, with varying endings.

Some epistles, again, seem to be addressed generally to Christians wherever they are — *James, 2 Peter, Jude* seem to be 'open letters to Christian brethren'. Finally, two 'epistles' appear to be sent to known groups within larger fellowships: *Hebrews* includes personal greetings, news, and the hope to be reunited with the readers, while urging them to obey those set over them (13:17-24); *1 John* reveals considerable knowledge of the readers ('my little children') and of the divisions among them (2:12-14, 19-21). Neither is addressed to a named location.

Despite their variety, however, all the New Testament epistles may share the description given to *Hebrews,* 'a word of exhortation' (13:22), provided that 'exhortation' is understood to include instruction, counsel, reminder, warning, explanation, answers to questions, as well as encouragement. The epistles are indeed pastoral counsel offered at a distance, and the general guideline to sound interpretation which emphasises the historical background of what is written applies to them as to every part of scripture. *They are of and for their time*, and some acquaintance with the circumstances and needs of the original readers, and the purpose of the writers, is essential to any intelligent interpretation of their timeless message.

To discover those circumstances and needs, we must first attend carefully to what each letter contains as a whole, and not discuss any text or paragraph on its own, as though it dropped like Diana of the Ephesians from the skies. Also, wherever possible, we must keep in mind the sketch of the founding of the church addressed, as given by

Luke in *Acts*. To read the epistles without *Acts* as their background is to forfeit any right to be heard on what the epistles mean. And thirdly, we must discover, and respect, what the writer is seeking to say and to accomplish, in each letter. Only the most cursory illustration of these points is here possible.

How the Roman church was founded is not known, though the presence of Romans at Pentecost probably provides part of the explanation. *Romans* is expressly designed to introduce Paul and his gospel to an influential church which he did not found and has not so far visited, so that the church may both welcome his coming and speed him on his way, with prayer, helpers and support, as he turns his face westwards to Spain (15:22–24). It appears that the Roman church regretted that he had been so long in coming to them (1:10–13); and that some in the church doubted the scripturalness, the ethical wisdom, and the consequences of his gospel of salvation by faith alone, and questioned his own loyalty to Israel, and his attitude to God's election of her. These are the points on which he explains himself. His 'visiting card' is therefore an extensive one, defending his mission and message against prevalent misunderstandings, though always with the very practical intent, that the readers may support his future plans.

1 Corinthians was Paul's response both to news about the church brought by several Corinthian visitors (1:11; 16:17), telling especially of the division of the church into parties, of serious immorality, and of disorder in their worship; and to a letter from the church enquiring about various matters (7:1) such as marriage, food offered to idols, his own apostleship, the gifts of the Spirit, the resurrection of Christ, and arrangements for support for poor Christians in Judea — all subjects on which, had Paul been present at Corinth, he would have given detailed instruction. (Recall Acts 18.)

2 Corinthians is mainly concerned with the aftermath of a serious disagreement between Paul and the Corinthian church, setting straight the record of his own actions and motives, explaining his own attitude towards the responsibilities of leadership, and resuming the collection for Judea, interrupted by the quarrel.

Galatians is a vehement, almost explosive, little epistle addressed apparently to the churches Paul had founded in 'the Phrygio-Galatian region' (Acts 13:51 to 14:23; 16:1–6), Lystra, Iconium, Derbe, amid opposition from local Jews. Paul has heard that the trouble has persisted, Jewish-Christian teachers persuading the Gentile Christians that they must keep the law of Moses as good proselytes to Judaism before they could enjoy salvation through Christ. This was an attack not only on Paul's converts, but on his gospel, his authority as an apostle, and his own Christian experience, for he had himself come out of strict Judaism to find salvation in Christ. Hence the sternness and indignation of Paul's reply, launching without greeting, thanksgiving or prayer into an assertion of his authority and independence, recalling the Galatians' beginnings in the gospel, and arguing for the replacement of the old bondage of the law by the freedom of the Spirit, sufficient guide and guarantee of Christian behaviour.

Ephesians is probably a circular letter, sent from prison (3:1; 4:1), celebrating Christian salvation, and designed especially to expound the ultimate divine purpose, to reduce a divided, fragmented universe to unity under the headship of Christ (1:10). The process has already begun in the raising up of the readers *together* in Christ, and in the reconciling of Jew and Gentile in one body, the church; it is to be carried forward by the ministry, within the church fellowship, in Christian homes, between master and servant, and in the warfare of the Christian against all evil. Paul's ministry to the district addressed is described in Acts 19 and 20, and in 2 Corinthians 1.

Philippians is a charming letter sent to the church of which Paul had happiest memories (see Acts 16:11–40). At the moment of writing, he awaits the court's verdict upon his life. The church had sent their pastor to him with a gift, and Paul now explains his total situation, thanks the church for their care, explains that their pastor had fallen seriously ill but is now returning; and bids the church cultivate the humblemindedness that cements and safeguards unity, and the continual joy which is the true tone of Christian life. The letter is strangely interrupted by a protest against trouble similar to that in Galatia; this leads Paul to a splendid confession of his own entire dependence on the righteousness given to faith by God in Christ.

Colossians is addressed to a church founded by one of Paul's converts (see 1:7,8; 2:1; 4:12), who on visiting Paul in prison (4:18) has reported that a strangely mixed heresy comprising elements of Judaism and features of gnostic philosophy was infiltrating the young church. Paul's reply meets head-on the implied denial of Christ's divinity with a wonderful assertion of the unique pre-eminence of Christ in the universe and in the church; but he dwells mainly on the fullness of Christ as divine Lord and Saviour in order to emphasise the fullness of life possessed by those who hold firmly to their first faith in him: they have no need to seek 'fuller' experience in alien teachings. Paul then describes how so sufficient a salvation should be worked out in personal character, communal life and worship, the Christian home, employment, the wider church, and towards outsiders.

The two letters to *Thessalonica* were sent from Athens and Corinth soon after Paul's visit, described in Acts 17. Persecution and bereavement have disturbed the infant fellowship, and problems have arisen over the expected early return of Christ, which is causing some unhealthy excitement and neglect of everyday duties. Paul recalls their fine beginning in Christian things, explains his teaching about the future, exhorts them to sober responsibility, and assures that the dead have missed nothing of the final glory of Christ.

1 and 2 Timothy and *Titus*, addressed to Paul's assistants, are devoted to instructions about church order and teaching, pastoral duties and discretion, encouragement and warning, with numerous detailed references to Paul's own career, movements, and expectation. In some respects, these so-called 'Pastoral Epistles' represent a Christianity much nearer to our own than does the rest of the New Testament: the church is becoming an organised society, with orders of officers and servants, including 'enrolled widows', carefully arranged finances, the faith summarised in 'faithful sayings' which ought to be held true, and 'a form of sound words' which pastors should 'have by them'.

Heresy is met with ridicule, abuse and warning, rather than with theological argument; the qualifications for Christian service are no longer the divinely bestowed gifts of the Spirit, but careful selection, ethical tests, and organised training. Moreover, perhaps the deepest change of all from earlier days lies in the recognition that a right faith and a transformed life can no longer be assumed to belong inevitably together. It cannot now be taken for granted that to believe in Christ *is* to be dead with him to sin, self, and the world, and to be filled with the Spirit. Now Christians must 'exercise themselves' to add right conduct to orthodox belief in a Christian life of good citizenship, true churchmanship, and responsibility. The exuberance, excitement and joy of the first Christian years have settled into steady Christian discipline of mind plus good behaviour.

The little letter to *Philemon* is a plea for

D

acceptance and forgiveness for a young slave who
ran away from his master (Philemon), apparently
stealing property as well, but who has met Paul in
prison and been converted. Paul therefore sends
Onesimus back with this intercessory letter to ease
his way into his master's trust and the church's
welcome.

The 'epistle' to the *Hebrews* resembles a treatise
more than a letter, though the final greetings and
news lend it an air of personal correspondence.
From a score of verses it is plain that the readers are
Christian Jews, under some pressure of
disappointment and persecution to return to the
safety and satisfactions of a legal religion, Judaism.
As we have seen, the argument of the epistle is that
Christians have much more in their new faith than
they could find in the old. Its appeal is intermingled
with the inspiration of past examples, and with
warnings of the dire consequences of apostasy.

James is something of an enigma. Debate continues
whether it is an early or a late production, by the
brother of Jesus or not, and for what purpose it was
written. Very significantly, its language and style are
only paralleled in the New Testament by the sayings
of Jesus himself, and perhaps the best interpretation
of the epistle sees it as a series of eight meditations
on the practical sayings of Jesus, designed to
recommend Christ's teaching to Christians and non-
Christians alike.

1 Peter is thought by some to have begun life as an
address to baptismal candidates: certainly the
earlier chapters expound the greatness of Christian
salvation, and appeal for loyalty to Christ, in a way
most appropriate for such a purpose. Peter's main
appeal is for submission — the opposite of sinful self-
will — towards public authorities, of servants to
masters, wives to husbands (with a warning to
husbands not to be inconsiderate), and all Christians
to one another and to God. The closing chapters

strike an increasingly clear note of coming suffering, as though the threat of persecution intensified during the writing of the letter. In some ways, 1 Peter is one of the richest portions of the New Testament.

Of 2 Peter and Jude, which cover much the same ground in much the same language, little can be said with assurance, except that they combat a gnostic heresy which teaches, among other things, that morality does not matter, and do so with energy and some strong abuse. 2 Peter seeks also to strengthen faith in the original gospel, and to assure that the purposes of God shall yet be fulfilled despite perplexing delay.

We saw that 1 John confronts a crisis of loyalties in the churches addressed, as gnostic teachers draw out once faithful Christians into private groups. 2 and 3 John are apparently personal letters, by an unknown 'elder' of the church, calling for discrimination, in the dispensing of Christian hospitality, between those who serve the truth and those who do not. On the other hand, unlikely though it seems, 'the elect lady' in 2 John 1 could mean a church, in good Greek usage.

Two controlling features of Revelation demand close attention, if overheated imagination, wilful fancy, and dogmatic nonsense are to be avoided. (a) It is an epistle addressed to seven existing churches, each intimately known to the writer in its history, strength and weakness, all in named towns and cities surrounding Ephesus (1:11; 2:1 to 3:22). Unless this is the most blatant and irrelevant pretence, the message of the book must have been intended for the members of those churches in their contemporary situation. (b) The book itself insists repeatedly that its message is for the time immediately succeeding its writing — 'What must soon take place . . . The time is near . . . I am coming soon . . . What must soon take place (again) . . . Do not seal up the words of the prophecy of this book for the time is near . . . I am

coming soon (again) . . . Surely, I am coming soon'
(1:1,3; 22:6,7,10,12,20). It is difficult to see how any
writer could insist more plainly than in these seven
warnings that what he has to say belongs to the
immediate future of the churches to which he writes.
Yet all through the centuries commentators have
ignored what is so clearly written, and have
pretended to find in the book a forecast of their own
times, or of some still distant future.

If we assume that the writer knew what he meant
(and if he did not, we need not trouble with the views
of lesser interpreters), then we must seek, with
whatever difficulty, the significance of his message
in the circumstances of his own and the immediately
succeeding time — in the struggle of church and
empire, probably about the end of the first century,
as Rome attempted to make the State itself the focus
of religious awe (the beast-idol with its 'priesthood').
Heroically, John calls for preparedness, for
resistance, and for martyrdom, in the strong
assurance that 'Babylon' — pagan Rome — would
certainly fall in ruins, to be replaced by the city of
God.

Such a call to underground resistance, from a
leader himself a prisoner of the State for his loyalty
to Christian faith, would be dangerous to possess:
hence the cryptic language in which references to
present rulers and policies are expressed. Some
clues familiar to the original readers are doubtless
lost to us. But through all the uncertainties there
shines a glowing optimism, a daring loyalty to Christ,
an unquenchable courage and assurance of victory,
such as the church in every age has needed to hear
again and again.

Even so cursory a summary of the circumstances
and intention of the epistles sets us at least at the
right point of view for a true, historical
interpretation. It demonstrates how closely involved
with the actual situation, the dangers, problems and

questions of the first Christians, these letters are. It
reminds us how 'occasional' the apostolic
correspondence was — written with no original
intention that it be read two thousand years later in
Christian worship in our very different world. Some
was not even preserved; the letter of Paul to
Laodicea (Col. 4:16), the earliest letter to Corinth
(1 Cor. 5:9) and the regretted letter also (2 Cor. 7:8)
are only those which we know to have perished.

Such a summary also illumines the actual
problems with which the epistles deal: the relation of
Christianity to Judaism, of grace to law, of faith to
works; the true assessment of Christ and his work;
the place of the Gentiles in the purposes of God; the
confrontation of Christian moral principles with
pagan conduct and custom; the real dangers of
misrepresentation of Christian teaching, especially
by the admixture of amoral libertarianism and
equally amoral intellectualism; the perplexing delay
of Christ's advent; and the problems of the
developing Christian organisation as ambition and
professionalism threatened spiritual vision and
dedication. These are not our problems to the same
degree: we have to set our problems alongside these,
and work out by the help of the Spirit what the
apostolic answers to our own difficulties might have
been.

From so many different writers, circumstances,
and needs arise the varied approaches to Christian
truth and experience which the New Testament, like
the Old, so richly represents. It is untrue to the
scripture, and self-impoverishing, to force all
meanings and insights into one rigid mould of
supposed 'orthodoxy', instead of letting each writer
bear his testimony in his own way. In the New
Testament, too, and perhaps especially in the
epistles, the precise language used becomes more
important to interpretation. Compared with Hebrew,
Greek is subtle, flexible, rich in vocabulary, and

there are more ways of saying anything available to
any writer. The way he chooses to express himself is
therefore always worthy of attention. For example,
Paul's 'I am not ashamed of the gospel of Christ'
(more precise translation than 'I am proud . . .')
implies someone had suggested that Paul would not
have the nerve to preach such a gospel in mighty
Rome! A carefully chosen word in 2 Corinthians 2:17
— 'We are not hucksters (peddlers) of the word of
God' ('hawking the word of God about' New English
Bible) reveals Paul's scorn for charges made at
Corinth that he preached the gospel for gain. In
Hebrews 12:1,2 the writer deliberately parallels the
race 'set before' us and the joy 'set before' Christ —
a striking nuance which the New English Bible
misses altogether.

To preserve humility, it is well to remember that
more intensive study of the apostolic writings reveals
a number of unsolved questions about which equally
competent and equally honest scholars can only
disagree. However uncomfortable and unfashionable
an open mind may be, it is the only reverent attitude,
not to say the only intelligent one, on some subjects.
For instance, nine New Testament books are
anonymous (including the four Gospels, despite
tradition), while there is nothing to show which of
several Johns, Judases, or James wrote the books
bearing those names. Every attempt to pierce this
anonymity is speculation, and no guess or theory is
more evangelical, or more Bible-loving, than any
other. We do well to be aware of our assumptions.

Further, scores of books or fragments exist — the
Apocalypse of Peter, the Gospel of Thomas and the
rest — which were published by Christians under
apostles' names, though never written by them. Paul
himself warns of 'a letter purporting to be from us'
whose teaching he repudiates — this, within his own
lifetime! (2 Thess. 2:2). In most cases, the real
author's intentions seem to have been laudable, to

remind the church of his own day of what this or that
master-teacher had once taught, and since the
substance was not the author's own, he attached to it
his teacher's name. But it follows that a book's claim
to be by a certain author is no guarantee that it is so.
Those best qualified to judge seem agreed that
tradition must be doubted as to the authorship of
John's Gospel, the Pastoral Epistles, *Hebrews*,
2 Peter and *Jude*; others wonder about *Ephesians*,
Matthew and *James*. It is surprising how little it
matters — so long as we do not let assumptions about
authorship govern our interpretation. The way that
Paul speaks about faith, sanctification, perfection,
and quotes Habakkuk, for example, must not control
our understanding of *Hebrews*, which uses these
words and others quite differently.

No reason can be discovered for the order of the
books in the New Testament. It is certainly not
chronologically arranged. This must be kept in mind;
careful reading will suggest several reasons why
2 Thessalonians would be more fittingly the first
written, and *1 Thessalonians* the second written,
after an interval, and to clarify some things in the
first-written letter. The lost two letters to Corinth
imply that our two letters are really *2 Corinthians*
and *4 Corinthians*.

But our *2 Corinthians* seems most disjointed and
contradictory. The story of the quarrel and its
resolution is begun in chapter 1, dropped at 2:13 and
resumed at 7:2 (or 5). The whole tone of chapters 2 to
8 is of rejoicing, explanation, conciliation, even a hint
of apology. Then, at chapters 10 to 13, the whole
quarrel seems to break out afresh as Paul pens some
of the sharpest, most ironical and self-defensive,
even accusatory language in the whole Testament.
The paragraph 6:14 to 7:1 seems wholly out of place,
too. All explanations are ultimately guesses: does
Paul turn to a section within the church (without
saying so)? or did he receive fresh news (without

saying so)? had he a sleepless night? Or is 2 Corinthians 10–13 part of the lost severe letter (2 Cor. 7:8); and is 2 Corinthians 6:14 to 7:1 part of the letter described in 1 Corinthians 5:9?

No one can be sure: though it is obvious a church might treasure whatever an apostle had sent them, using the same piece of expensive papyrus to copy whatever they possessed, and never intending the whole to be taken as one letter. What became of the beginning and ending of the fragments, in that case? A similar explanation could throw light on the strangeness of *Philippians* which begins with news of Paul's circumstances, passes to exhortation, resumes news of their pastor's welfare, breaks off to castigate Judaisers, returns to more exhortation and finally, very belatedly, says 'Thank you' for their gift. *Perhaps* here, too, several notes have been copied together.

The questions posed by the Pastoral Epistles are manifold. The occurrence in them of over three hundred words not found elsewhere in Paul's letters is surprising: did he learn a new vocabulary in old age? But we may recall that most of his epistles were dictated, whether because of poor eyesight (Gal. 4:15; 6:11), custom, or his own ease of composition: and the amount of freedom given to his 'secretary' to put things in his own language would vary greatly. The change of tone, of counsel (for example about marriage), the greatly developed church organisation, the authoritative stance and the new way of meeting heresy with condemnation in place of discussion, are all harder to place in Paul's lifetime. Most difficult of all is to fit the various movements of Paul and others, mentioned in these letters, into Paul's career as outlined elsewhere. But we simply do not know the story of Paul's last years.

The commonest guess, that after the house-arrest of Acts 28 Paul was released, toured the east again, visiting Colossae, Crete, Ephesus, and Philippi, was re-arrested, taken to Rome, wrote to Timothy and Titus, and was martyred, is sheer speculation, though it *could* be right. It is based almost wholly on the desire to fit the Pastoral letters into his lifetime. Such a story left no trace at all on the New Testament, or on early Christian records; and it contradicts Paul's announced expectation (Acts 20:25,38 — Why did Luke let this stand if it was not true?), and his declared plans, based on insight into God's will (Rom. 15:18–29). Moreover, such a guess makes the end of *Acts* inexplicable — it would so well have suited Luke's defensive purpose, if he could have told of Paul's release at that point. As against all this, the alternative guess, that the Pastoral letters comprise notes written by Paul to Timothy and Titus at various points during their service of him, is equally speculative, and would be very difficult to prove. We should, again, be aware of the assumptions we are making, whenever we try to interpret any passage against an uncertain background.

One further puzzle that requires mention concerns the 'prison' epistles. The traditional presumption that the fleeing Onesimus would make for Rome hardly stands examination with a map in hand: Ephesus is far more likely, given all the circumstances. The further assumption, that the 'Praetorian Guard' and 'Caesar's household' show that Paul wrote *Ephesians*, *Philippians*, *Colossians* and *Philemon* from his imprisonment in Rome is likewise unsound: the Praetorian rank was in fact an imperial civil service, represented in every 'Government House' throughout the empire, and even at Jerusalem (Matt. 27:27). It becomes then an open question *which* imprisonment these letters date from: and it resolves some difficulties if we understand that *Colossians* and *Philemon* were written from an imprisonment in Ephesus (unrecorded, but note 2 Cor. 1:8–11; 1 Cor. 15:32),

and possibly the Ephesian circular too; and
Philippians at a later date from Rome. Paul's
intention to revisit Philemon would not then conflict
with the plans announced in Romans 15. But this, too,
is speculation.

Some Bible readers find such uncertainties
irritating and accuse those who raise them of 'want
of faith' — as if piety, or faith, can possibly resolve
historical questions! The truth is, that such
difficulties emerge relentlessly, when one disciplines
oneself 'to read what is there', instead of what one
has been taught to see there. Once more, a little
humility aids interpretation, or at least forestalls
dogmatism.

The realisation that the epistles comprise pastoral
counsel to the *churches* underlines a further feature
— the amount of Christian knowledge which they
presuppose. Not conversion only, and the basic truth
of the gospel, are assumed, but the sacraments,
church life, leadership, the mission of the church to
the world, an elementary syllabus of ethical and
religious teaching widely used as 'the traditions',
'the pattern of sound words', 'the standard of
teaching to which you were committed' (2 Thess.
2:15; 2 Tim. 1:13; Rom. 6:17). The duties required in
the epistles presuppose the saving grace of Christ —
they are not its precondition. The epistles' contents
are Christian education, not evangelism, the
subsequent analysis of Christian experience, and of
church life, not its first proclamation. Modern
evangelism too often uses the language and the
theological complexities of the epistles in presenting
the gospel to enquirers. The epistles should certainly
help the *evangelist* to understand the gospel: they
should not be imposed upon the unevangelised, as
preconditions of salvation.

Finally, interpretation of the epistles is greatly
helped if we remember that the New Testament
represents an 'interim report' upon many subjects

still under active discussion as the canon closes. Understanding, and divine revelation, arise within debate, sometimes. In *Galatians, Colossians,* 1 Corinthians 12–14 (on the Spirit), Paul may be seen actually 'doing' theology, arguing out still deeper insights, still wider implications as he wrestles with the challenges and the denials confronting the infant churches. In the epistles we are privileged to overhear a debate in progress. A living church — and the New Testament church is certainly that — must also be a thinking church, whose faith and thought are never at rest but in movement, exploring its own experience, listening to the Spirit, looking for answers to each new problem life presents. Thus the New Testament resembles a 'still' photograph taken out of a rolling film; or better, a botanical slide or section, a thin slice cut across a living plant stem for microscopic examination: the one thing the microscope cannot show is the life still going on.

Christian reaction towards the State, for example, changes as the New Testament proceeds (as we have seen), and so does Christian thinking about the delayed return of Christ. The apostolic church is still thinking out, as the New Testament closes, the relation between general immortality (the resurrection of just and unjust, to reward or judgement) and the gift of eternal life to those only who 'have the Son' — who believe. And the church, no less clearly, is still discovering all that is implied by identifying the Spirit of God as the Spirit of Jesus: to watch the development of the Church's understanding here, is most rewarding. On the breadth of the church's mission, too, and on the application of Christian ethics to new problems in a non-Jewish, pagan environment, the church was still finding her way as the apostolic age closed.

To the end huge questions remained unanswered, while many that troubled the later church and still trouble us had not yet been raised. On some subjects, the New Testament records the stage which Christian exploration and experience had reached at that time. To imagine, or to invent, a final date for the closure of divine revelation, in order to induce a certainty which we crave for but do not possess, is to fool ourselves. The New Testament offers no ground for the assumption that all was said which God wanted to say, by around AD 100. The fact that the New Testament now has a back cover must not mislead us: 'the Lord has yet more light and truth to break forth from his word' as the old Puritan assured the Pilgrim Fathers.

This raises several far-reaching questions, which must not be evaded if our interpretation of scripture is to be of living use to us. To these we now turn.

7

Guidelines for Contemporary Interpretation

Among the sharpest of the many comments of Jesus
upon the ways of religious people is the charge that
they are sometimes too fond of their Bibles to listen to
the voice of God. In a study of biblical interpretation
that warning must not be evaded.

The occasion was an accusation of blasphemy
against Jesus, because he 'called God his father,
making himself equal with God'. Jesus replied that he
was totally dependent upon the Father, who himself
bore testimony to him. The trouble was that the Jews
had never heard his voice, did not have his word
abiding in them, and so did not recognise God's
testimony, or believe him whom God had sent. 'You
search the scriptures, because you think that in them
you have eternal life; and it is they that bear witness
to me; yet you refuse to come to me that you may have
life' (John 5:18–40).

Jesus evidently expected that a knowledge of the
scriptures would prepare a man to hear the living
voice of God, the word that God was speaking to that
generation. Instead, devotion to the written scripture
had come to displace attention to the contemporary
word of God; they were missing what God was saying
by arguing about what God had said, long ago. It is

sadly possible to know and love the Bible yet remain
deaf to the divine approach to ourselves; to believe
very firmly that 'God has spoken', but not that he still
speaks.

Jesus was much concerned over this deafness and
blindness of his generation to what God was saying
and doing in their time. The sap was rising in God's
trees, he suggested; it was a time of fulfilment, a day
of visitation, and Jewry knew it not. The kingdom was
amongst them, the finger of God was stirring that
age, the disciples were blessed above many to have
witnessed what prophets and kings had longed to see
and had not seen. Many were longing, even praying,
for the Day of the Lord, completely unaware that
they were living in it, unable to read the signs of the
times or the impending changes in the spiritual
weather.

So Jesus reiterated in a dozen ways the appeal that
so haunted the mind of a later writer also, 'Today if
you will hear his voice, harden not your hearts'; 'he
that hath ears to hear, let him hear'. It is a treble
tragedy, a sore irony, if the one thing that stops our
ears to the word God wants to say is our
determination to hear nothing that he has not
already said, centuries ago.

Insistence upon a strictly historical approach as
the pre-requisite of interpretation and the foundation
of all Bible study tends to strengthen the temptation
to think of all divine revelation as remote in time and
far removed in circumstance from our own day and
situation. Setting every passage of scripture in its
historical context, as a stage in a long-past and
slowly developing divine self-disclosure, always
stressing its primary relevance to its own time,
inevitably appears to minimise scripture's relevance
to our time, and problems, and questioning. Loyalty
to scripture becomes concentration on the past;
though the reason for our emphasis on the historical
approach is to exclude fanciful, private,

uncontrolled interpretation, its effect, with some people, is to raise a serious question whether the Bible can then be the final authority on all matters of faith and practice for the modern Christian.

The answer must be that the God of the Bible still speaks: the scriptures contain no *finished* word of God. Several lines of thought converge to warn of this. (i) The fact that the New Testament itself records an unclosed, ongoing discussion on many points reinforces its own teaching that revelation continues. The New Testament opens with a sixfold assertion that understanding of the truth moves forward: 'You have heard that it was said of old time . . . But I say to you'; and it practically closes with the appeal, repeated seven times, 'He who has an ear, let him hear *what the Spirit says* to the churches.' That seems to preclude any idea that God had spoken for the last time.

(ii) The reminder that the early church existed and flourished for two centuries without an 'authorised' New Testament forces us to realise that Christian instruction and direction are available elsewhere, not *only* in the scriptures. The all-important truth here is that the apostolic church was engaged, so to speak, in writing the Gospels and epistles, while living meanwhile under the inspiration, direction and superintendence of the Holy Spirit. This is the picture of the early church which Luke describes so vividly, and which Paul analyses in his account of the Spirit in the life of the believer (Rom. 8) and of the church (1 Cor. 12 to 14) — and everywhere else.

Jesus had promised repeatedly that the Spirit would direct and empower the disciples, giving them wisdom and words by which to answer persecutors (Matt. 10:19,20). In John's Gospel, this 'intellectual' ministry of the Spirit is fully elaborated as the coming to the disciples of the Spirit of *truth*, to dwell in them, to teach them all things, to bring to their remembrance all that Christ has said to them; to

bear witness to Christ alongside the disciples'
witness, so convincing the world of sin,
righteousness and judgement; to say the things that
Christ had to say if only the disciples could have
borne them; to declare the things that are to come,
taking of the things of Christ and declaring them to
the disciples (John 14:17,26; 15:26,27; 16:7–15).

Here is a clear, and immensely significant promise
of a teaching ministry that recalls and illumines the
past, guides in the present, and opens up the future,
a ministry of the Spirit by which the church shall live
and witness in the hostile world. Such continual
ministry of the Spirit in teaching and guiding the
ongoing church must never be undervalued, *least of
all on the plea of loyalty to scripture.*

Yet it does for many earnest minds create a
tension between the once-for-all revelation, written
down, carrying 'final' authority for all time, and the
promise that the Spirit will guide believers into all
truth. The importance of such a tension may be
illustrated, historically, in the growth of an
authoritative, over against a charismatic, ministry,
the 'authorities' appealing to the written word alone;
in the quenching of inspired Christian prophecy in
favour of the Christian scribe expounding inspired
documents, with an obvious loss, sometimes, of
immediacy and relevance. Of course there are perils.
No Christian desires angel visitants disclosing more
golden plates and magic spectacles. Yet something is
lost in a Christianity for ever looking over its
shoulder to the distant past for the guidance it needs
for the present. The apostolic church did not do that.
And both the changing situation of the Christian, and
the inexhaustible richness of Christ, suggest that no
set of documents, however indispensable and
precious, could capture and define for all time his
infinite significance for history and for mankind. We
do need that the Spirit shall take of the things of
Christ and reveal them unto us, in age after age after
age.

(iii) The Reformed faith has always held that the ultimate ground of Christian assurance is the illumination of the truth by the Spirit within the heart of the believer. The record of revelation is not itself the experience of revelation: the *experience* occurs within the soul of the reader reverently listening for the word of God to himself within the record of God's words and deeds in the past. Truth must dawn upon the soul, shining by its own light, self-authenticating by its source, its ring of authority, its reasonableness, its results in healing, inspiring and enhancing life. So Jesus spoke to Peter at Caesarea Philippi of the blessedness of such inward revelation, which does not depend upon 'flesh and blood' but is directly from the Father in heaven.

And so too Calvin looked for the corroborative witness of the Spirit within the hearts of those who read the Bible, the authenticating Spirit on the one hand and the scriptures on the other being two aspects of God's self-revelation. Other writers in the strongly Protestant tradition distinguish two senses in which the Bible is the word of God: as the record of what God said in other times, and as the vehicle of God's word to our own time. 'Faith is listening to scripture as the word of God'; not as a compendium of doctrines, nor as the testimony of others to what God said to them, but as the word of God 'hidden in the scripture' and speaking directly to us. In this way, Bible study becomes in truth an encounter with the living, speaking God.

And this is, after all, the ultimate goal of all our interpretation of scripture: not a well-stored mind, but a personal experience of divine instruction, guidance, illumination, forgiveness and enrichment. There is very little practical value in investigating an ancient revelation unless it becomes also a revelation to myself. Only so does the Bible become, to me, in any intelligible sense, the word of God.

Nevertheless, to many Christians this emphasis upon a continuous and contemporary word from God will sound dangerous, as opening the way for deviations from the original gospel, and as a setting aside of scriptural teaching in favour of 'new truth'. In particular it may be objected that the word of God was given, complete, once for all time, for Christians in the New Testament; that the authority of scripture is and must be final, or we are lost in uncertainty and confusion; and that in any case we are being offered in place of objective divine truth a subjective and fallible human judgement on what is the word of God in and for our own time.

Such caution is right, and very necessary, and the objections are well taken. But the promises of the New Testament remain; the need for a continuing knowledge of God in our own terms for our own time remains; the promise of the Spirit's continual teaching remains; the warning that love of the Bible may itself supplant the living word of God *to us*, likewise remains.

Where does truth in this matter really lie?

(a) The objection that the word of God was given, complete, once for all, for Christians in the New Testament, needs to be very carefully stated. Neither the facts, nor their implications are quite so simple — they are indeed surprising. For the New Testament was never formally closed, by any divine revelation or by any widely representative church council. For three-and-a-half centuries the church debated whether certain of the New Testament books should be included among the scriptures read in public worship, and whether certain other books, often bound with these, ought not also to be 'canonised'. In the end it was the prestige of two great individuals, Augustine (in a private letter) and Jerome (by deciding what to include in his received Latin — 'Vulgate' — translation) which 'settled' the New Testament, so far as it has ever been settled. Down to, and after, the Reformation argument continued about the authorship and value of certain books. Luther criticised *James* as a 'right strawy epistle', and drew a line between certain New Testament books and others apparently of lesser value and authority, in his eyes. Calvin doubted the authenticity of *2 Peter, James* and *Jude*, and omitted *Revelation* from his commentary, though he used the book as part of the existing Bible.

In practice, of course, the church has recognised the authority which lies within the twenty-seven books which now comprise the New Testament, and by so doing conferred an ecclesiastical authority also upon them. The very informal way in which that recognition was reached is usually balanced by the claim, made in faith, that the Spirit was superintending the whole process through the mind of the church. Most Christians would say that: but we must then be careful what conclusions we draw from it. We cannot on the one hand claim the authority of the Spirit for the selection of scripture *and* on the other hand appeal to the scripture to silence the continuing voice of the Spirit.

A great New Testament scholar has likened the closing of the New Testament canon to drawing a line beneath the apostolic age, as though God has 'said his say' for all time when the last of the New Testament books was added. This would suggest that God withdrew from the world when the apostolic age came to an end, and has no longer anything to say to those who diligently seek a word from the Lord. This view can scarcely hope to nourish a living faith, or satisfy the longing for clear Christian guidance relevant to today's complex problems.

The only consistent attitude would seem to be one that reverences deeply the canonised scriptures as the record of a revelation given long ago in unrepeatable events and lives, *and at the same time* looks to the illumination of the Holy Spirit in the present day to make that revelation intelligible, contemporary, and powerful, and still to lead us into all the truth, as Jesus promised.

(b) What, then, has become of the 'finality' of

scripture? The perpetual danger of being trapped by our own words faces us here as everywhere. 'Finality' needs very careful definition, if it is not to rule out altogether the later ministry of the Spirit in the church, and we must make some essential distinctions. The final authority of the Christian scriptures over the Christian mind and ministry means (i) that on whatever issues the New Testament clearly pronounces, what it says is for Christians unchallengeable, settled, beyond argument. Discussion will proceed on the precise bearings of the scriptural pronouncements, on how to express them in contemporary terms, on how to apply them to modern situations: but their essence and meaning will be accepted. Examples would be countless: the personal incarnation of God in Christ, and his limitless significance for humanity; the saving efficacy of his death and resurrection; the supremacy of love and the divine law; the demand for obedience to the Lordship of Christ; the value of prayer; the assurance of forgiving love; the promise of the Spirit to all who believe — and many such New Testament principles which are the basis of Christian thought and experience. Indeed, it is the unquestioning acceptance of such teaching as unarguable that makes such thought and experience 'Christian'.

The final authority of the Christian scriptures over the Christian mind and ministry means (ii) that on whatever issue the New Testament discussion is left unfinished, what it does say is for Christians directive. A clear example is the slowly emerging new attitude, within the New Testament, towards slavery. The institution of slavery is not confronted in the Gospels, but immediately poses a problem as the church moves out of Jewry into the Gentile world. A head-on attack upon the system was impossible: in the great centres of population, slaves heavily outnumbered free men, and Rome would allow no faintest attempt at organising liberation-movements. Nor did the Christian gospel regard a man's social position as all that important.

But the slave was — so the epistles insist — 'one for whom Christ died', and when he was a believer, then he was wholly a brother, Christ's free man, bought with the same precious blood as other Christians, loved and welcomed; masters were to treat their slaves fairly, giving them all that was just and equal, knowing that they too had a Master in heaven — with that demand for justice, equality, and treatment as in the Lord's sight, all that was most objectionable in slavery was destroyed. The slave was sent forth into the world with an inner dignity and a sense of personal worth to Christ and to the church which enabled him to 'walk tall' — while still a slave. And Paul insists also that he carries the same moral responsibility to work faithfully and honestly as all free men bear. Doubtless it took far too long for the New Testament directives to work out to the total abolition of slavery from any 'Christian' society, but the discussion continued *in New Testament ways* in changing conditions, until a clear obligation to set all men free was realised.

On the place of women in the Christian church, on the Christian attitude towards the State, and on Christian duty in time of war, the church has likewise taken a long time to digest, understand, and apply what the New Testament says; often because its teaching is obscured in the Christian mind by other, non-scriptural motives, but sometimes because the discussion within the New Testament was itself inconclusive, as on the precise scenario of the after-life. But in any attempt to state 'the Christian view', the New Testament remains the starting point and the guide: the discussion proceeds in the direction the New Testament was taking.

The final authority of the Christian scriptures over the Christian mind and ministry means (iii) that on

whatever issues the New Testament does not plainly
pronounce, its principles remain nevertheless
normative. Such issues would include surgical
abortion, organ transplants, genetic engineering,
artificial contraception, nuclear and germ warfare,
and many others that obviously did not arise for the
apostolic church. Upon such questions we have to
make what judgements we can; citing biblical verses
is of very little help, and sometimes scarcely honest.

'Normative' here means at least two things: we
shall search sincerely and diligently within the
scriptures for whatever moral and spiritual
principles we can honestly claim to be relevant to
such new modern problems, and strive to argue
reasonably and persuasively towards a coherent and
Christian attitude. It is not difficult, for example, to
take one's stand upon the whole biblical doctrine of
creation of the world by God, pass to the affirmation
that 'the earth is the Lord's, and the fullness thereof',
and on these build a scriptural attitude towards the
new issue of conservation of natural resources and
the care of the inheritance we leave for our children.

It is harder, on many modern problems, to
interpret fairly the scriptural bases from which new
attitudes may be formulated, though the sacredness
of life itself, in the eyes of him who created and
redeemed it, is a firm starting point on several
issues. But the sincere attempt to work from within
the scriptural world in order to find norms of
behaviour for our so different world, is an
acknowledgement of the authority of scripture over
our ways.

The other meaning of 'normative' here applies
when we fail to find any such starting points within
scriptures for the problems that confront us
(excluding freakish and untruthful interpretations of
texts that have nothing to do with their original
meanings), and have to frame a Christian attitude
without scriptural help. (The conception of the child

outside the womb might be such a totally non-biblical situation.) But even then, we shall acknowledge the authority of scripture in our sincere desire that nothing in our final decision about such matters shall be inconsistent with known scriptural teaching, when fairly interpreted.

The final authority of the Christian scriptures over the Christian mind and ministry means (iv) that on whatever issues God has still something to say to us, the teaching of the New Testament will prove to have been *preparatory*. In one respect, of course, this is speculative. What form will the second coming of Jesus take? By what means will the kingdom of God be ultimately realised? What will life in heaven be like? On such matters, all we can truthfully claim is that when it comes to pass, we shall find the scripture has come true! But this is precisely the case with the more important Old Testament prophecies: the fulfilment illuminated the prophecies more than the prophecies illuminated the future. When Jesus had come, lived, and died, the promise of the Servant of the Lord who should bear the sin of many was at last understood.

In another respect, the confidence that whatever new things God will say to us will prove to have been prepared for in the scriptures is of real value. Many Christians fear any suggestion of 'new and further revelations': those who know Christ to be the living and perfect word of God will not expect any new, 'contemporary' word to be at variance with him, but instead some new emphasis, new approach, fresh insight into his fullness of meaning, a new and urgent *force* in things about him that we thought we knew.

Such was the new revelation of the wholeness of Christ that came to Paul as he took the Jewish Messiah to the Gentiles; such the fresh understanding that came to St Francis as in Christ's name he set free the heart of Christendom to sing and laugh again; such the radical new insight that came to Luther as he rediscovered Christ as the sinner's only Saviour; such the totally renewing power that burst upon John Wesley, the liberating vision that kindled William Carey ... In each instance, the essential truth was old as the Gospels: but who will doubt that God spoke anew in each soul, and with driving urgency? It is not a *different* word from God that we long to hear: but a living and revitalising word; when it comes we shall recognise it as already prepared for in the word we have heard already, and its credentials will be those we always meet in Christ's teaching — authority, relevance, novelty, self-evident truth, and Christlikeness.

Thus on no subject, old or modern, will the Christian feel free to disregard what the New Testament says. He cannot claim it is always sufficient, for there are problems on which it speaks no clear and unmistakable word: but he will feel bound whenever possible to argue forward from New Testament insights to applications that could never have occurred to the first Christians, as he seeks to transplant discipleship from Palestine and the first century to the 'global village' of the twentieth.

(c) This brings again into sharp focus the third objection to any talk of new and contemporary revelation: the objection that in the end we are left with only fallible, subjective, human judgement as to what is the word of God for our time. The only possible reply is that such earnest Christian judgement is exercised upon what is *given* in the literature revered by those who stood nearer to Christ in time; it is a judgement controlled by constant appeal to the mind of Jesus himself, so far as his mind and spirit can be discovered from the documents that enshrine his memory; and it is a judgement deliberately surrendered, in humility and by prayer, to the guidance of the Holy Spirit.

(i) By judgement, as to what God is saying to me, 'exercised upon what is *given*' to me in scripture, we mean it is a selective, not a creative judgement: it does not invent its own scriptures, but studies those we inherit. Whatever I say God has spoken to me will ever be in line with the original historical meaning of the word, not a defiance of it. Consistency with past truth is not necessarily bondage to it, but it is a necessary safeguard.

What is at stake here may be illustrated by contrast with a widespread and well-intentioned religious movement of some years ago, which sought a revitalised and 'immediate' Christianity by fostering (among other things) the practice of guidance, understood as waiting upon God with notepad, pen and empty mind until God gave directions for the day. Here, perception of the revelation given was (in theory) wholly subjective, a matter of inner feelings; in practice, many adherents drew upon previous Christian training to sift the impulses that arise from the vacant or the subconscious mind.

The Society of Friends, in a somewhat similar way, looking for the 'inner light' of the Spirit, would give smaller place to the *control* of any guidance received by scripture's teaching than would most evangelical Christians. It is as antidote to the admittedly great dangers of mere feeling, impulse, human intuition, fondly mistaken for 'leadings of the Lord', that the serious Bible student turns to his scripture for an external, objective, inherited source of truth, while devoutly praying that by the ministry of the Spirit of truth that external truth will become *also* the light of God within his soul.

ϒ In practice, this means that because God is the same in all generations, what he said and did in certain biblical situations he will say and do with me, in so far as my situation resembles the biblical one. What God said through Paul to a quarrelsome church in Corinth, he says still to every quarrelsome church. What, according to Psalm 73, God said to one heart bitterly envious of the prosperity of wicked men, he says to me when I resent the comfort and success of the careless or the evil-minded around me. What Jesus said in the Upper Room to disciples fearful of the future, he says to me when I am afraid of the coming years; and what he said to the Pharisees about their self-righteousness, he says still to me, about mine. What '1 John' wrote to people who made high spiritual claims but were lacking in faith and love, God says to me if I resemble them.

Every biblical situation that can be repeated in my life finds its relevant word within the scriptures. Time is telescoped: we place ourselves into the situation described within the sacred page, and the truth comes alive. More often, indeed, as every Bible-lover can testify, the Bible reaches out to lay hold of us, and places us, whether we will or no, into the target area, saying 'Thou art the man!' When our situation resembles only slightly that of which we read, then the word that came to them becomes the clue to what God would say to our own different circumstance. In all this, I am not inventing what God says, nor merely putting my own thoughts into scriptural language: I am listening, observing, pondering what God *has* said, and with due reverence for its original meaning, I am discerning what God therein is saying still. The given, inherited revelation is 'homing' on my heart.

(ii) By judgement, as to what God is saying to me, 'controlled by constant appeal to the mind of Jesus himself', we mean that without hesitation or hedging, in everything, within scripture and outside it, our loyalty as Christians is to Christ. The judgement we exercise is not our own. Because Christ is the word of God incarnate, because he is the Bible's theme, centre, and gift, because as Luther said, the Bible is the cradle wherein Christ was laid — Christ is its Lord and judge. Thus the supreme guideline for a Christian interpretation of all scripture is: Christ, the Lord of scripture.

This is no vague, pious aphorism, but an extremely practical principle. It means that we judge everything in the Old Testament and the New by his mind and spirit. Through the whole thousand years of the Old Testament story, the movement flows steadily towards Christ, and so we can, and must, leave behind anything — food laws, battle scenes, poison cup trials, family feuds, harsh expressions in the Psalms — that proves in the end to be alien to his mind and spirit. Similarly, all the New Testament flows from him, the history of the early church, the letters of his disciples, the attempts to express his meaning in new and pagan terms: all is therefore set in his light, and by him we evaluate everything said and done, before we receive it as God's direction to ourselves.

So, if we do find anything even within the New Testament out of harmony with Christ's mind and spirit, we leave it aside, out of loyalty to him, as but part of the fallibility of the church, the immaturity of disciples. Many will insist that there can be no such thing — and insist without looking! Whether we find anything in apostolic words or attitudes below Christ's standard will depend on what we make of — for examples — Paul's apparent motive for doing good to enemies, 'by so doing you will heap burning coals upon his head'; the attitude to opponents expressed in the Pastoral Epistles (1 Tim. 1:20; 2 Tim. 4:14), so different from 1 Corinthians 13; the abuse expressed in 2 Peter; the coarseness of the rebuke offered to Judaisers (decently disguised in RSV of Gal. 5:12); Paul's remnants of racial pride, and his ambivalent attitude towards women. When Paul himself distinguishes between 'the word of the Lord' and 'I say' (1 Cor. 7:8,10,12), and tells us he regretted some things he had written (2 Cor. 7:8), there seems no reason why we should disagree with his own judgement.

But what matters is not our decision about such

details, or our agreement or disagreement with one another about what we think is truly Christlike: these are questions of individual maturity. What matters is the recognition of where the final authority in scripture lies, and of that Christians can hardly be in doubt: it is the mind and spirit of Jesus, as these are revealed in the Gospels. He — not our own subjective judgements — is the Lord and arbiter of scripture.

(iii) By judgement, as to what God is saying to me, 'deliberately surrendered to the guidance of the Holy Spirit', we mean that in this task of thinking forward from the New Testament and transplanting its teaching into the modern world, the Christian is not left to his own wisdom, or scholarship, or experience, or 'hunches', but is aided by the promised Spirit of truth.

In the areas of history, languages, background information, skill in interpretation and translation, doubtless the promise that the Spirit will guide into all truth does not apply. A diligent, cautious and teachable mind is the only key to *learning*. But discovering the meaning of scripture for our own lives involves also something of moral wisdom, shrewd judgement, understanding of character, knowledge of oneself, the patience to learn from our own and others' experience, the humility to consult Christian friends, and an obedient will. In this realm, most of all, 'unto him who has shall more be given'.

Just because the qualifications for understanding God's truth and ways are not primarily intellectual, it is not reverence and piety merely, but intelligence and sound judgement which advise that we remember at all times what it is we are interpreting, and why; and so remembering, approach the work with humility and with prayer. Only so is room made, amid our many assumptions, preconceptions, and uncertainties, for the Holy Spirit to 'take of the things of Christ and show them' unto us. As it is the pure in heart who see God, so it is the humble in heart who

hear him, and the meek whom he guides in judgement. Only such a receptive spirit comes truly to appreciate the wisdom, the spiritual power, the searching truth and the satisfying richness of the word of God.

It is the purpose of the Bible to perpetuate for every generation the revelation of God given to Israel and in Christ. It is the ministry of the New Testament in particular, under the tuition of the Spirit of truth, to reproduce in generation after generation of Christians, the mind of Christ. That is the aim, and the supreme reward, of all biblical interpretation. To attain it, no labour, and no care, can be too great.

Conspectus of Old Testament History, Saul and after:

About 1051 BC
(One kingdom)

Prophets:

Saul (40 yrs)
1 Sam. 9 on, 1 Chron. 8 on — Samuel was prophet, then
David (40 yrs)
1 Sam. 16 on, 1 Chron. 11 on — Samuel and Nathan:
Solomon (40 yrs)
1 Kgs. 1 on, 1 Chron. 29 on — Nathan (at first)

[Divided kingdom: about 931 BC]

North, Israel
Jeroboam (22 yrs)
1 Kgs 12 on, 2 Chron. 10 on

South, Judah
Rehoboam (17 yrs)
1 Kgs 11 on, 2 Chron. 9 on
Abijam/Abijah (3 years)
1 Kgs 14 on, 2 Chron. 12 on

Nadab (2 yrs) 1 Kgs 14 on
Baasha (24 yrs)
1 Kgs 15 on, 2 Chron. 16
Elah (2 yrs) 1 Kgs 16
Zimri (7 days) 1 Kgs 16: 8 on
Omri (12 yrs) 1 Kgs 16: 16

Asa (41 yrs)
1 Kgs 15, 2 Chron. 14 on

Ahab (22 yrs)
1 Kgs 16 on, 2 Chron. 18 — Elijah in north; followed
Ahaziah (2 yrs)
1 Kgs 22 on, 2 Chron. 20 — by Elisha; Micaiah also during Jehoshaphat's
Jehoram/Joram (12 yrs)
2 Kgs 1 on, 2 Chron. 22 — time (1 Kgs 22:5 on)

Jehoshaphat (25 yrs)
1 Kgs 15 on, 2 Chron. 17 on